THOMAS NAYLOR'S
PATHS TO
PEACE

SMALL IS NECESSARY

LOCAL PATHS TO PEACE TODAY, VOL. 2

COMPILED AND EDITED BY
WILLIAM L. BENZON

Thomas Naylor's Paths to Peace: Small Is Necessary

Copyright © 2019 William L. Benzon. All rights reserved. No part of this book may be reproduced or retransmitted in any form or by any means without the written permission of the publisher.

Published by Wheatmark®
2030 East Speedway Boulevard, Suite 106
Tucson, Arizona 85719 USA
www.wheatmark.com

ISBN: 978-1-62787-628-5 (paperback)
ISBN: 978-1-62787-629-2 (ebook)
LCCN: 2018951192

Contents

Preface: The Kairos Radical Imperative
Thomas Naylor..1

What's in This Book and Why
Bill Benzon 7

Foreword: Naylor's Arguments in a Broader Context
Charlie Keil..13

A Vision for Us All
Larry Chisolm and Charlie Keil..21

The Middlebury Declaration
Kirkpatrick Sale and Thomas Naylor 29

The Life and Ideas of Thomas H. Naylor—
An Interview 33

The Principality of Liechtenstein:
A Model of Self-Determination for a World Filled with Chaos
Thomas Naylor...67

A Community of Small Nations for a Sustainable Planet
Thomas Naylor...73

Self-Determination for Small Nations
Thomas Naylor...79

The Case for the Self-Determination of an American State
Thomas Naylor 83

Untied States of America
Thomas Naylor 87

Swiss-Like Direct Democracy in America
Thomas Naylor 89

Secession Fever Spreads Globally
Thomas Naylor 95

The Montpelier Manifesto
Thomas Naylor 103

The Eerie Silence of American Lawyers, Clergy, and Academics in Response to the Empire
Thomas Naylor 111

Thomas Naylor, RIP
Kirkpatrick Sale 115

Afterword: The Pull Factors
Charlie Keil 123

The Books of Thomas Naylor 131

Live life to the fullest and try to die happy.
—Thomas Naylor, May 30, 1936–December 12, 2012

Preface:
The Kairos Radical Imperative

Thomas Naylor

Editor's Note: This is one of the very last things that Thomas Naylor wrote—he died, unexpectedly, a month later—and is thus, in effect, a final plea for us to come to our senses.

> *Kairos*: A Greek word for a very special time fraught with decisive consequences for good or evil when momentous things are happening, new possibilities arise, more degrees of freedom emerge, and the opportunity to seize the moment appears. A time for renewal and nonviolent action when the forces of light rise up against the forces of darkness.

So said German theologian Paul Tillich shortly after World War I. With the emergence of "religious socialism" in Europe, Tillich saw what he thought was a kairos, according to theologian Robert McAfee Brown: "a time that God was seeking to use, and to which humanity was called upon to respond—an historical era in which a new *political* order responsive to religious concerns, and a new *religious* sensibility deeply immersed in the political order, could join forces." Unfortunately, this kairos did not come to be or went unrecognized by Europeans. Rather, the European experience included Adolf Hitler, the Holocaust, World War II, and the Cold War—not a pretty sight.

Although it was Tillich who popularized the word *kairos* in the twentieth century, kairos reemerged in Latin America in the 1960s and in South Africa in the 1980s. In Latin America, it was closely linked to what became known as *liberation theology*.

Inspired by the Second Vatican Council (1961–65) and Pope Paul VI's 1967 encyclical *Populorum Progressio* (On the Progress of Peoples) but grounded in the widespread poverty and violence in Latin America, a radical form of Christian theology emerged in the 1960s called *liberation theology*. The main thrust of this new theology was a "preferential option for the poor." Within a few years after its inception, liberation theology spawned thousands of small lay-led Christian communities throughout Latin America. Many of these so-called base communities (*comunidades de base*) literally had their origins in small-village Bible study groups that stressed not Catholic doctrine but community action aimed at solving very real social and economic problems. Some coalesced around very specific projects, such as digging a well, building a road, negotiating with wealthy landowners, and defending the village from guerrilla attacks. Above all, base communities were not passive. Indeed, they were often made up of political activists who some called revolutionaries.

Many villages owned collective farms as well as collective stores, pharmacies, health clinics, and schools. In other villages, families owned their own small plots of land. Base communities fostered an atmosphere of cooperation, trust, and sharing, as well as a strong sense of community.

Unfortunately, Latin American base communities became victims of their own success. Wealthy landowners, conservative Roman Catholics, and right-wing military governments found the community action and direct democracy practiced by base communities to be threatening. Under pressure from Pope John Paul II, Vatican power broker Cardinal Joseph Ratzinger, and the Reagan administration's foreign policy in Latin America, the Catholic Church withdrew its support for base communities in the 1980s and began distancing itself from liberation theology.

Before he became Pope Benedict XVI, Cardinal Ratzinger was John Paul II's hatchet man. He was responsible for leading the war against liberation theology and enforcing Catholic dogma worldwide. Among the prominent Catholic theologians investigated and disciplined by Cardinal Ratzinger were German theologian Hans Kung; left-wing California priest Matthew Fox; Belgian priest Jacques Dupuis; Brazilian liberation theologian Leonardo Boff; and Peruvian priest Gustavo Gutierrez, who actually coined the term "liberation theology."

In response to antidemocratic John Paul II and his henchman Cardinal Ratzinger, a group of liberation theology leaders signed the Central American Kairos on April 3, 1988:

> A chance for grace in which the Lord calls us to take up the challenges of this historic hour. A chance for grace to create a new international order where right makes might and not vice-versa, where peoples who have been denied and humiliated through the centuries become free human beings, to live in sovereignty and self-determination,

where small nations can live together in brotherhood and sisterhood without any Empire threatening them.

But once again kairos was not to be. Pope John Paul II and Ratzinger, along with their fascist-friendly allies in the Catholic organization known as Opus Dei, ripped out the heart and soul of modern Christianity. Stripped of liberation theology, Christianity became the religion of George W. Bush and his Christian fundamentalist and Jewish neocon friends. John Paul II and Cardinal Ratzinger did irreparable damage to Christianity in general and to the Roman Catholic Church in particular. "What would have happened, Guatemalans and El Salvadorians ask to this day, if Ratzinger and Pope John Paul II had regarded the Latin American call for liberation from autocratic rulers with the same force with which the European churchmen supported the Polish Solidarity revolution?" wrote journalist Mary Jo McConahay for Pacific News Service.

However, a document known as *The Kairos Document*, published in South Africa on September 25, 1985, did have a much more salutary outcome. It is credited with having contributed to the end of apartheid a few years later.

But what about today? Have we not arrived at our very own kairos? We, the citizens of the United States and the rest of the world, find it increasingly difficult to escape the clutches of the largest, wealthiest, most powerful, most materialistic, most environmentally irresponsible, most racist, most militaristic, most violent empire in history that does little to support the vast majority of its citizens or any other citizens than its own superrich. We are haunted by the nihilism of separation, meaninglessness, and powerlessness and subsumed by political elites who use corporate, state, and military power to manipulate our lives. We have become mere pawns of a global system of dominance and deceit known as *technofascism*, in which transnational megacompanies and megastates control us through money, markets, technology, and media, sapping our political will, civil liberties, collective memory, traditional cultures, sustainability, and independence. We are all victims of affluenza, technomania, cybermania, megalomania, globalization, and imperialism.

Isn't it high time we respond to the radical imperative of this kairos by seizing the moment, assuming responsibility for our lives, confronting the American empire, and taking control of our own destiny? Do we really have any other choice than to reject the immoral, corrupt, decaying, dying, failing American empire and seek its rapid and peaceful dissolution before it takes us all down with it?

Recognizing that the United States and the other meganations of the world have become so large that they are unfixable, should we not work diligently to (1) discredit them whenever possible, (2) seek their rapid and peaceful dissolution before they destroy the planet, and (3) encourage the development of small, sustainable, nonviolent, socially responsible, self-determined, meaningful communities and small nations everywhere?

If we choose to ignore the sense of urgency and radical imperative associated with this kairos, we do so at the risk of great peril!

November 11, 2012

What's in This Book and Why

Bill Benzon

While Thomas Naylor published his ideas in a number of full-length books, he also wrote many shorter pieces, many of them for web publication. This collection is based on those pieces and on a long interview with the *Daily Bell* in 2012. This interview situates his ideas *in the context of* his life, making it ideal for this book, which Charlie Keil and I conceived as a pamphlet-sized handbook for provoking and promoting thoughts about downsizing the nation and, consequently, upgrading people's control over their lives. As such, we have organized *Small Is Necessary* into bite-sized chunks that can be read in short stretches of time—while waiting for a bus, for the tea to cool down, in moments of refreshment after watching the birds at the feeder, or even in a moment of quiet frustration while locked in a traffic jam on the interstate during a holiday weekend.

This collection consists of a number of those smaller pieces, including two manifestoes, a somewhat rearranged and edited version of the interview, and opening and closing essays in which Keil places Naylor's ideas in anthropological and ecological contexts. Most importantly, it is designed so that you can read it in small chunks. The interview has been rearranged so that it is more coherent, and a few relatively small sections have been dropped (we've provided the online address for the full interview). The resulting collection thus unavoidably has some duplication.

So if you find yourself reading something you've already read, just skip over it and move on.

Unless otherwise indicated, all pieces are by Thomas Naylor.

Preface: The Kairos Radical Imperative: here Naylor links his ideas to those of Paul Tillich and liberation theology in Latin America and later South Africa.

Foreword: Naylor's Arguments in a Broader Context, by Charlie Keil: Keil indicates a cosmic context ("we live in a unique galaxy"), a philosophic context (a "paradigmatic shift in conscious" is necessary), and a natural context ("think globally act locally"), all leading toward the self-determination of peoples and persons.

A Vision for Us All, by Larry Chisholm and Charlie Keil: eight sets of principles, goals, and actions in support of the vision outlined in this book.

The Middlebury Declaration, by Kirkpatrick Sale and Thomas Naylor: a call to action from 2004: "To this end, therefore, we are pledged to create a movement that will place secession on the national agenda …"

The Life and Ideas of Thomas H. Naylor—an Interview: Naylor discusses his ideas in the context of his life. His early life was in the Deep South (Mississippi), and he ended up in Vermont in search of community. He taught economics at Duke, the University of Wisconsin, Middlebury College, and the University of Vermont. In the 1970s, he ran SIMPLAN Systems, a fifty-person software firm, and consulted with the major corporations and the governments of over thirty countries, including extensive trips to the Soviet Union, Poland, Hungary, and Czechoslovakia. This essay includes a chronology of the contemporary Vermont secession movement, comments on sustainability, Ron Paul, and the American empire, and ends with four steps to the future: denunciation, disengagement, demystification, and defiance. "By far the most difficult step in the process of deciding to embrace secession is the emotional one of letting go of one's images of America as *the home of the free and the brave* and *the greatest nation in the world*."

The Principality of Liechtenstein: A Model of Self-Determination for a World Filled with Chaos: Liechtenstein is a tiny nation in the Alps that Naylor sees as a model of how good small can be. Hans-Adam, the ruling monarch, believes that "citizens should not be seen as servants of the state, but rather as customers of a benevolent service company, otherwise known as the state, whose aim is to serve its customers."

A Community of Small Nations for a Sustainable Planet: Naylor believes that "it is high time for the smaller nations of the world to begin withdrawing from the United Nations" so that they can form a Small Nations' Alliance (SNA). They would act as role models "encouraging others to decentralize, downsize, localize, demilitarize, simplify, and humanize their lives" while calling for the "nonviolent breakup of the United States, China, Russia, India, Japan, and the other meganations." The founding group might include Denmark, Finland, Norway, Sweden, and Switzerland and grow to include Costa Rica, Senegal, and Bhutan, among others.

Self-Determination for Small Nations: "Self-determination is an act of separation or withdrawal from a larger body." It is common for individuals—leaving home, ending a relationship, etc.—but seems problematic for larger political bodies. It shouldn't be. Self-determination is a step on the way to having one's higher needs (in Maslow's sense) fulfilled. However, it does involve loss, and loss is difficult, but necessary and inescapable.

The Case for the Self-Determination of an American State: Naylor presents twenty propositions outlining the conditions and responsibilities of an American state, such as Vermont, seeking to separate from the nation. Number 18: "Radical nonviolence can undermine power and authority by withdrawing the approval, moral support, and cooperation of those who have been dealt an injustice. It derives its strength from the energy buildup and very real power of powerlessness."

Untied States of America: Naylor suggests that the United States should devolve into twenty small nations, each internally more coherent than the current nation-state.

Swiss-Like Direct Democracy in America: Switzerland is another paradigm case for Naylor. With a population of over seven million people, it is considerably larger than Liechtenstein at thirty-five thousand. "Direct democracy works in Switzerland because Switzerland is a tiny, well-educated, hard-working country with a strong sense of community. The United States is not Switzerland …. Although introducing direct democracy into the United States sounds like a very good idea, it would involve a number of conceptual, legal, constitutional, economic, technical, and political challenges. Such a move would require bold, creative political leadership combined with world class marketing skills." Alas, the United States may be too large to govern coherently.

Secession Fever Spreads Globally: One of Naylor's strongest arguments is the simple fact that the move for self-determination is growing, with roughly 250 political independence movements at the time Naylor wrote this in December 2012. Naylor takes us on a quick tour of these movements. "According to the *second law of thermodynamics*, heat will always flow only from a hotter object to a colder object. More generally, the direction of spontaneous change in isolated systems of all sorts is always toward maximum disorder. This concept is known as *entropy*. Therefore, it is hardly surprising that large, highly centralized, undemocratic nations such as the United States, China, Russia, and India are starting to come unglued at the seams and will eventually descend into chaos. [...] We are truly entering unchartered waters. Past trends are meaningless."[1]

The Montpelier Manifesto: This is signed by Thomas Naylor, Kirkpatrick Sale, James Starkey, Challis Glendinning, Carolyn Chute, and Charles Keil. It sets forth the case for Vermont's secession from the United States and was released online in the fall of 2012 and read at the Third Statewide Convention for Vermont Self-Determination on September 14, 2012. It is organized under several headings:

- *Document of Grievances and Abuses* (in Governance, Economy, Foreign Policy, and Civil Liberties)
- *Criminal Justice* (millions of people imprisoned and the failed "war on drugs" that costs billions)
- *Social Services* (inadequate health care, education, and social-welfare net)

---

1 See *Wikipedia* article, "Self-determination," for an overview with pointers to more specific information: https://en.wikipedia.org/wiki/Self-determination

- *Infrastructure* (highways, bridges, tunnels, airports, dams, levees, public water—all failing; transportation crises)
- *Redress of Grievances*: "Let us therefore consider ways to peaceably withdraw from the American empire by (1) regaining control of our lives … (2) relearning how to take care of ourselves … and (3) providing democratic and human-scale self-government at those local and regional levels most likely to affect our safety and happiness."

The Eerie Silence of American Lawyers, Clergy, and Academics in Response to Empire: Those three groups made significant contributions to the civil rights movement and anti-Vietnam War movement. Where are they now? "With such an important part of our country's intellectual firepower sitting silently on the sidelines, we are actually in a far worse position than might first appear. We are morally, spiritually, and intellectually bankrupt."

Thomas Naylor, RIP, by Kirkpatrick Sale: "Thomas Naylor … was an extraordinary man, and his spirit and his influence will be missed by many."

Afterword: The Pull Factors, by Charlie Keil: "Big is bad, unstable, and bound to fail, but how small do we have to go to be good, safe, sane, and successful?"

Foreword: Naylor's Arguments in a Broader Context

Charlie Keil

First, some frameworks, contexts for understanding the importance of Thomas Naylor's contributions to the Great Transition and a paradigm shift in consciousness: (1) cosmic, (2) philosophic, (3) green or natural, and (4) self-determination of peoples and persons and the liberation of nations; peoples; cultures; and persons/individuals, especially women and children, currently trapped in obsolete state formations.

Cosmic Context

Our universe is unique. We live in a unique galaxy within a unique solar system on a unique planet that supports a unique coevolution of millions of lifeforms. Our unique species, *Homo ludens collaborans*, has coevolved thousands of unique cultures, languages, music, myths, rites, and modes of social being and will, hopefully, coevolve still more thousands of overlapping languages and dialects, musics, dances, rites, and myths—plus unique cultural patterns of primary and secondary communication processes currently called "performing arts" and "writing/visual arts," respectively.

Philosophic Context

The paradigmatic shift in consciousness that I believe must take place soon is from all kinds of dismal alienations from nature, society, body, labor, and mind back to joyous participation in nature, society, play, performing arts, and mindfulness. This shift can also be thought of as a shift in emphasis from current epistemologies (ways of knowing the world and owning that knowledge) to future ontologies (ways of being in the world) and celebrating that merging of mind and body, self, and "other" individual in society, mind in nature players playing games for the fun of it rather than the winning and losing. Albert Camus and existentialism were Naylor's avenue to these participatory philosophies. Soon a revived paganism, polytheism, infinite varieties of local animist, pre-Socratic, and post-Socratic provocation will reunite religion and philosophy in thousands of different local paths to local Edens.

Green or Natural Context

The Ten Key Values (p. 26–27) proposed some decades ago by the Green movement continue as the framework for Green Party efforts to decentralize all over the world. There are probably more "greens" per capita in the Green Mountain state of Vermont than in any other US state, but Naylor, like Kirk Sale, rejected the Green Party assumption that the American two-party system could be rejected or replaced by a new Green majority in the foreseeable future. Still, all ten of the Key Values match up well with Naylor's thinking that small is necessary and not optional.

I am continually pushed back to the Green slogan: "Think globally, act locally." As modified by Mark Dickey, slinging some insightful slang, "Chill globally, groove locally." The main pull, I believe, will come from dancing, singing, drumming, sounding, miming, pantomiming, puppetizing, joking, charading and parading, dramatizing, worshipping, praising, rites of passaging, and playing out our dreams in pursuit of happiness right/wright here. And write/rite now. It's a much better use of local food and local energy to have fun, love thy neighbor as thyself, and follow "peace is the way" every day. It may be as simple as rejecting the two major men's oppressors: "bringing home the bacon" and "kill or be killed on command." Men, resolve never to go to "work" or to "war." Women, don't take on men's oppressions and call it liberation. We/they, LGBTQs, and XYZs, notice that work and war are run by antidemocratic "chains of command."

Self-Determination of Peoples and Persons Context

Bernard Nietschmann's article "The Third World War: Militarization and Indigenous Peoples"[2] sets the stage for whole shelves full of books, one or more books for any one of the three-thousand-plus nations suppressed or attacked by the roughly 195 to 200 currently recognized states. When Nietzschmann talks of nations, he uses an understanding common in anthropology:

> Nations are geographically bounded territories of a common people ... who see themselves as "one people" on the basis of common ancestry, history, society, institutions, ideology, language, territory and (often) religion ... The existence of nations is ancient.

---

2 *Cultural Survival Quarterly* 11, no. 3 (1987), pp. 1-16.

In contrast:

> A state is a centralized political system, recognized by other states, that uses a civilian and military bureaucracy to enforce one set of institutions, laws, and sometimes language and religion within its claimed territories. This is done regardless of the presence of nations that may have preexisting and different laws and institutions. States commonly claim many nations that may not consent to being governed and absorbed by an imposed central government in the hands of different people.

In these terms, then, Nietzschmann argues that states have been warring with nations since the end of World War II:

> The Third World War has already begun. It began when states tried to take over old nations. It began in the hills south of China and north of India and Burma. It began in 1948. Burma moved its army into the Karen and Shan nations and India started its military invasion of the Naga nation. The Third World War is now being fought on every continent except Antarctica. It has produced millions of casualties and massive forced dislocations of nation peoples who make up the majority of the world's refugees. It encompasses most of the peoples and groups who are accused of being terrorists. Each year it involves new areas, states and nations.

Following this paragraph, there are many brief but vivid

descriptions of persecuted and frustrated nations within dozens of states: "States such as Indonesia that stretches across 3,000 miles, 13,700 islands, and 300 nations," writes Nietzschmann. And I know from two visits and two and a half years of personal experience that many of the 250 to 300 nations within Nigeria—some of them already further separating into Christian, Islamic, and pagan versions of what had once been a single cultural and linguistic group—would like to be independent or to be democratically confederated differently in five, six, or something like a dozen states of various sizes. Thirty to forty million Hausa might form an actual and very rare entity: a nation-state. Yoruba speakers might be happier in a loose confederation of polytheistic and democratic city-states. Biafra could be revived and thrive, or break into an Igbo confederation and a coastal confederation. Naylor's writings in his last year collected here make various eloquent appeals to the small nations of the world to unite in transitioning and rebalancing our world ecologically, socially, politically, and economically.

The practical importance of Thomas Naylor's work, as I caught up with it in the year before he died, (December 12, 2012) may be considered, in the medical model, threefold:

(1) Naylor's Diagnosis: We need to appreciate the depth, breadth, and brevity of the Montpelier Manifesto (p. 47–51). As an economist, Naylor tells us clearly what is so wrong, wrong, wrong, and wrong again about technofascism and the failing debt/deficit burdening the American empire, or "global economy."

(2) Naylor's Prognosis: Naylor begins to explain what will happen and what it will take to make everything right/rite/wright/write again for self-determination of peoples and persons on this one and only planet that has sustained a miraculously balanced

coevolution of millions of species and many thousands of cultures over many millennia ... up until very recently.

(3) Naylor's Cure for What Ails Us: Hear the call to kairos (p. 103) and to rebel nonviolently. Respond at all levels: person by person, one friendship group at a time, one community ...

street by street and block by block
from taz[3] to PAZ, with a minimum of culture shock.

That is, from temporary autonomous zones to permanent autonomous zones, as in permaculturing food and having a modest but reliable, sustainable, and very local energy supply. It is on these local peace economy bases that we can create tens of thousands of new cultures and crafts in tune with Mother Nature—econiche by econiche, stream by stream, watershed by watershed, bioregion by bioregion.

In the technofascist era, millions of Americans are in deep denial over the many wrongs that need to be made right. I believe the most important challenge before us is to create irresistible visions of the fun, the play and pleasure, and the deep satisfactions we will enjoy from collaborating with each other and with Mother Nature to build up both local peace economies and wilderness paths, corridors, and areas that can sustain a lasting diversity of species, as well as a rebirth of egalitarian societies with cultures to match—all over the planet.

---

3 Hakim Bey advocated for the creation of "temporary autonomous zones," hence "taz." TAZs are social spaces that elude established social hierarchy. PAZ is Spanish for peace.

Kirkpatrick Sale, cosigner of both the Vermont Manifesto (2003) and the Montpelier Manifesto (2012), describes here (p. 103), and elsewhere,[4] the inexorable push toward decentralization and "human scale," but has less to say about the pull. So let's talk some more about that pull right here (and in our afterword (p. 123), anticipating a fuller treatment of this topic in volume 3 of this peace series.

In mid-November, a month before December 12, 2012, Naylor posted "The Kairos Radical Imperative" (p. 1) as both a history of the concept and a call to action, followed two days later by a postscript (p. 111) asking, "Why don't we hear clergy, lawyers, and academics raising the alarm?" Six years later, summer of 2018, the answer is clearer and simpler than it was six years ago: fear. Fear of nuclear war. Fear of drones. Fear of phones. Fear of five or more kinds of weapons of mass destruction. Fear of many thousands of addictive "weapons of mass distraction." Fear of being shot by an NRA-inspired vigilante. Fear of being run over by a car, truck, or van during a march or demonstration. Fear of becoming a victim at a big party or a concert or a nightclub. Fear of not being allowed to come up for tenure. Fear of never being invited to a parish position. Fear of being labeled an extremist, radical, rabble-rouser. Fear of not having a career. Fear of not having a day job or part-time employment. Fear of torture. Fear of being revealed as a coward. Fear of becoming a hypocrite, talking the talk and then not walking the walk. Fears, and more coming, in every nook and cranny of societies these days.

Or, for those who have been on the sidelines—witnessing,

---

4 *Human Scale* (New York: Coward, McCann & Geoghegan, 1980).

spectating, not taking a stand, not speaking up—anxiety and depression. Passive fear and quiet paranoia: soul destroy'ya. Fear takes many silent forms. And many of the traditional sources of faiths that used to combat fear have been corrupted. For many years I took comfort from Harvey Jackins's assertion of "benign reality," the sun rising each morning and supplying all the energy our global speciation needs in just the right proportions. After centuries of corruption and pollution of our air, water, and soil, even this fundamental benign reality is now in question.

For our own souls, for restoration of self-respect, for a way out of the current crises and into a sane and joyous future, we urge you to read this book and volume 1, *We Need a Department of Peace: Everyone's Business and Nobody's Job*. Use your reasoning powers and your conscience to find your place in a local peace economy that desperately needs outspoken citizens to encourage each other and inspire our doctors, lawyers, 'Indian chiefs', academics, freelance journalists, musicians, poets, madmen, and specialists, to speak out, twist and shout, honk and bonk, pick and sing, and oh yes, shake that thing. As you do this, look for guidance from the following:

> *Ninth Amendment to US Constitution*: "The enumeration in the Constitution, of certain rights, shall not be construed to deny or disparage others retained by the people."

> *Article One of Universal Declaration of Human Rights*: "All human beings are born free and equal in dignity and rights. They are endowed with reason and conscience and should act towards one another in a spirit of brotherhood."

A Vision for Us All

Larry Chisolm and Charlie Keil

The earth is alive. All forms of life are interdependent. Violence against one another and violence against the earth that sustains us now threatens to destroy much of the world. For our own sake and for our children and our children's children, we need to develop ways to stop the destructive forces and to turn our energies toward making a good life possible for everyone on this beautiful planet—all of us in our sweet diversity and for the fullness of our days. We invite you to consider our common situations and to reconstruct our futures, possibly along lines suggested by the following principles.

1. Equalize world life
   Modern society is dominated by values that socialize people from birth into attitudes that objectify, quantify, and control. This value system results from a history of male dominance in which aggression, competition, and hierarchy are encouraged while emotion, cooperation, and intuition are not. This underlying theme links together the problems we face in the world today. As a result, women must struggle for the rights that protect and safeguard their bodies, their sexuality, and their livelihoods. The natural world and all its inhabitants have been lumped into an aggregate of quantifiable objects whose existence is subject to extinction, belittlement, or denial according to the self-interest of a privileged few. The rigid

dichotomies we have created between masculine and feminine, white and nonwhite, heterosexual and homosexual, rich and poor, fuel the oppressions that keep people from developing to their fullest potential and are reflected in our cultural patterns, bad habits, and socially approved addictions.

GOALS: Eliminate domination, discrimination, and persecution on the basis of sex, color, class, sexual preference, religion, or age by identifying our individual complicities in the old patterns and creating the supportive conditions for each of us to change the world, beginning with ourselves. Commitment to processes that create social norms and values that are more holistic, ecological, and egalitarian.

2. Demilitarize and democratize world life
World military expenditures in 2018 approached $1.7 trillion.[5] The USA alone is now spending over $68 million *every hour* on further militarization. This expense, not only in money but in human energies, creativity, and intelligence, is at best producing products that are never used and at worst produces instruments that kill, maim, torture, and coerce us. Military production is economically and ecologically destructive, producing no true wealth, only illth and filth. Under the might of armaments (most of them supplied by the big powers) the peoples of the world (most of them very poor) live under coercive regimes. Militarization thrives on

---

[5] Stockholm International Peace Research Institute, accessed Sept. 13, 2018, https://www.sipri.org/media/press-release/2018/global-military-spending-remains-high-17-trillion.

fear, trains unquestioning obedience, intimidates critics of established injustice, and "legitimates" rule by force. This violence spills over into all facets of life. All this is unworthy of our great human intelligence and can be stopped.

Democratize because people everywhere deserve to participate in decisions that determine the conditions of life such as access to food, shelter, health care, and the quality of life that only small face-to-face communities of equals can give. The social and economic structures of nation-states bar access through hierarchies of privilege and ideologies that support domination by class, race, gender, age, and nationality—all backed up by coercion.

GOALS: Violence-free areas and a violence-free world in which the concept of violence is redefined to encompass all the things that block the self-sufficiency of individuals and communities. Education empowering people with knowledge of all options and belief in the reality of a daily life with peace and justice. Conversion of our military industries into the life-enhancing technologies of peace and ecological sanity.

3. Decentralize world life
   The large nation-states are squandering the world's resources on militarization and holding us all hostage to nuclear terror. We must find ways out of these political and economic arrangements. Without trying to predict the role of world government; the new boundaries of bioregions; or the emergence of self-determined zones, cities, and islands, it is clear that

moving local communities toward ever greater political and economic self-sufficiency is the only decentralization process we can do something about here and now.

GOAL: A world safe for the rediversification of democratic cultures and protected against the reemergence of nation-states and empires.

4. Clean air, clean water, clean food, clean earth
   Our planet is being poisoned without our consent by herbicides, pesticides, and toxic materials that reach us at work, at home, and at play.

   GOALS: Poison-free areas. Establish, expand, link-up. Encourage whole food enterprises and organic farms. Support community, worker, and consumer rights to know about toxins and alternatives. Stop the throwaway society—recycle and repair.

5. No more radiation beyond natural forces
   Radioactive materials make us sick, kill us, and mutate us. There is no harmless level of additional exposure to radiation. All stages of the nuclear fuel cycle and all phases of nuclear weapons manufacturing and storage endanger all forms of life adjacent and worldwide.

   GOALS: Radiation-free zones without nuclear weapons, nuclear power plants, or nuclear wastes. Establish, expand, link up. Support safe public power, conserve all energy, encourage the use of renewable energy—solar, wind, geothermal, or hydro—appropriate to each region.

6. Support and develop good livelihood and good health
   Put energies into work that promote good living; produce nothing that demeans the maker, the user, the recipient, the earth. The wholeness of individual and social life is the context for health.

   GOALS: Worker-owned and -operated enterprises, for example, food co-ops for production, storage, distribution, and marketing. Decentralize and buy local products. Extensive gardening and local food production in every inhabited part of the earth is the basis for all true security. Support exports of surplus *only* after basic needs of region's peoples are met.

   Free medical care and education: local clinics and home care; training in medical self-help; public health education and practice; worldwide health insurance for everyone.

7. Support ecological and cultural diversity
   Because extinction of species is accelerating and each extinction is irreversible. Because every culture lost is lost forever. Life depends on diversity of species interacting.

   GOALS: Support wilderness areas worldwide to insure species survival. Support land-based indigenous peoples worldwide. The knowledge of indigenous peoples is essential to continued life on earth. Their claims to control the conditions of their life on their lands are just; all our lives depend on justice.

8. Network actively
   Communicate "prime-arily" and transnationally with others

of like mind, especially by dance, music, songs, poems, stories, fairs, festivals, rites, ceremonies, barter, stylized expressivity of all kinds, living toward a world that is peaceful, diverse, healthy, socially just, full of joy, and mutually respectful of all our children's futures in the infinite generations to come.

GOALS: Establish and/or support transnational organizations of personal growth, educational, and cultural exchange—sister city, town, village, county projects, etc.

This set of eight principles, goals, and actions was written by Larry Chisolm (1929–1998) and edited for the Buffalo Greens by Charlie Keil (and updated a bit in 1997 and 2015) as they got organized in the mid-1980s. It was originally called "Vision for Buffalo & the Niagara Frontier" and was meant to complement the four principles articulated by the worldwide Green Movement:

  (1) ecological balance
  (2) grass roots democracy
  (3) nonviolence
  (4) social justice

And to be in agreement with the "Ten Key Values," as phrased by the Green Committees of Correspondence in the USA:

  (1) ecological wisdom
  (2) grassroots democracy
  (3) personal and social responsibility
  (4) nonviolence

(5) decentralization
(6) community-based economics,
(7) postpatriarchal values
(8) respect for diversity
(9) global responsibility
(10) future focus

The Middlebury Declaration

Kirkpatrick Sale and Thomas Naylor

Whenever any form of government is destructive of these ends [life, liberty, and the pursuit of happiness] it is the right of the people to alter or abolish it, and to institute new government in such form as to them shall seem most likely to affect their safety and happiness.
—*Declaration of Independence*

We gathered here this weekend to explore the possibilities of a new politics that might provide a realistic and actionable alternative to the familiar sorry political scene around us that has just ratified its decadent and corrupt nature with the reelection of George W. Bush. We are convinced that the American empire, now imposing its military might on 153 countries around the world, is as fragile as empires historically tend to be and that it might well implode upon itself in the near future. Before that happens, no matter what shape the United States may take, we believe there is at this moment an opportunity to push through new political ideas and projects that will offer true popular participation and genuine democracy. The time to prepare for that is now.

In our deliberations, we considered many kinds of strategies for a new politics and eventually decided upon the inauguration of a campaign to monitor, study, promote, and develop agencies of separatism. By separatism we mean all the forms by which small political bodies, dedicated to the precept of human scale, distance themselves from larger ones, as in decentralization, dissolution, disunion, division, devolution, or secession, creating small and independent bodies that rule themselves. Of course, we favor such policies that operate with participatory democracy and egalitarian justice, which are attainable only at a small scale, but the primary principle is that these states should enact their separation and self-government as they see fit.

It is important to realize that the separatist/independence movement is the most important and widespread political force in the world today and has been for the last half century, during which time the United Nations, for example, has grown from 51 nations in 1945 to 193 nations in 2004. The breakup of the Soviet Union and the former Yugoslavia are recent manifestations of this fundamental trend, and there are separatist movements in more than two dozen countries at this time, including such well-known ones as in Aceh, Basque country, Catalonia, Scotland, Lapland, Sardinia, Sicily, Sudan, Congo, Kashmir, Chechnya, Kurdistan, Quebec, British Columbia, Mexico, and the Indian nations of North America.

There is no reason that we cannot begin to examine the processes of secession in the United States. There are already at least twenty-eight separatist organizations in this country—the most active seem to be in Alaska, Cascadia, Texas, Hawaii, Vermont, Puerto Rico, and the South—and there seems to be a growing sentiment that, because the national government has shown itself to be clumsy, unresponsive, and unaccountable in so many ways, power should be concentrated at lower levels. Whether these levels should be the states or coherent regions within the states or something smaller still is a matter best left to the people active in devolution, but the principle of secession must be established as valid and legitimate.

To this end, therefore, we are pledged to create a movement that will place secession on the national agenda, encourage non-violent secessionist organizations throughout the country, develop communication among existing and future secessionist groups, and create a body of scholarship to examine and promote the ideas and principles of secessionism.

Middlebury, Vermont, November 7, 2004

The Life and Ideas of Thomas H. Naylor—An Interview

Editor's Note: Anthony Wile conducted an interview with Thomas Naylor and published it in *The Daily Bell*, May 13, 2012, under the title "Thomas H. Naylor on Leviathan, Secession and Vermont's Small Nation Dream." The interview took the form of numbered questions from Wile followed by responses from Naylor. I have edited the review by rearranging some of the materials and in some cases removing material that is more adequately handled elsewhere in this volume. While I have rearranged Naylor's remarks, I have retained the question numbers from the original interview in case you may want to look it up on the web. Consequently the numbers you see below will not always be consecutive. I have also added descriptive subheadings to guide your through the topics.

If you want an overview of Naylor's thinking set in the context of this life, this is the single best source for you. The interview is available in its full original form on the web: https://www.thedailybell.com/all-articles/exclusive-interviews/anthony-wile-thomas-h-naylor-on-leviathan-secession-and-vermonts-small-nation-dream/

In Search of Community: From Mississippi to Vermont
1. *Daily Bell: Can you give us some background on yourself?*
   I grew up in Jackson, Mississippi, in the 1950s, where my

father admonished me to "be cautious" and always be concerned about "what people will think." I was never very cautious nor very concerned about what people thought. I used to refuse to stand when Dixie was played at Ole Miss football games, and I understood fully the significance of that decision.

After three years at Millsaps College, I moved to the Great Satan, New York City, and entered Columbia University, where I earned a BS in industrial engineering. Two years later, I received my MBA from Indiana University. Summer jobs at International Paper Company, Sun Oil, and Dow Chemical convinced me that corporate America was not for me. At IU I became interested in computers, which played an important role in my life for the next twenty years.

In 1961 I began teaching management science at Tulane University while working on my PhD in economics. Upon completing my PhD, I joined the faculty of Duke University, where I taught economics, management science, and computer science for thirty years. For six years I taught all the courses in corporate strategy at Duke's Fuqua School of Business.

In 1969 I cofounded the LQC Lamar Society, an organization of progressive young southerners committed to the premise, ironically, that the South should return to the Union, get off the race kick, and start solving its own problems. By 1972 all the important progressive political leaders in the South, black and white, were members of the Lamar Society. Some of them included Jimmy Carter, Winthrop Rockefeller, Terry Sanford, Julian Bond, Maynard Jackson, and Andrew Young.

During the 1970s I was president of SIMPLAN Systems,

a fifty-person computer software firm whose clients included Fortune 500 companies such as General Motors, United Air Lines, McDonald's, IBM, Shell Oil, Texaco, Monsanto, Pacific Gas & Electric, and Kuwait International Petroleum. I was a strategic management consultant to major corporations and governments in over thirty countries. The happiest day of my life was when I sold the company to a bunch of Germans for a profit in 1979.

As a result of the fact that the Russians illegally published one of my books on computer-based planning models and free market models in the Soviet Union in 1974, I received a steady flow of Soviet and Eastern European visitors to Duke until 1991. This gave rise to a 1982 visit to Moscow for a preview of perestroika three years before Gorbachev came to power. My book was being used to build computer simulation models to evaluate the effects of introducing free market capitalism into the Soviet economy. Throughout the 1980s I made frequent visits to the Soviet Union, Poland, Hungary, and Czechoslovakia. In 1985 I married a Polish psychiatrist. My life would never be the same.

Between 1982 and 1991, I became a self-appointed, unpaid cheerleader for Gorbachev, whom I considered to be the greatest political leader of the twentieth century. During this period, *The New York Times* published several of my pieces about the Soviet Union.

On the evening of January 16, 1991, ten minutes before the bombing began in Baghdad, William H. Willimon, dean of the Duke Chapel, and I launched a freshman seminar on "The Search for Meaning." Three years later Willimon, my wife, Magdalena, and I published a book bearing the same title. This was the first of five books Willimon and I would coauthor, the last of which was *Downsizing the USA* in 1997.

In 1993 my wife, son, Alexander, and I moved to Vermont in search of community. We found it. Vermont is different—very different. It is all about the politics of human scale—small towns, small businesses, small schools, and small churches.

Vermont provides a communitarian alternative to the dehumanized, mass-production, mass-consumption, overregulated, narcissistic lifestyle that pervades most of America—an alternative to the politics of money, power, speed, greed, gridlock, and fear of terrorism.

Recognizing that the United States had become more like its former nemesis the Soviet Union than most Americans care to admit, in 2003 I founded the Second Vermont Republic, a nonviolent citizens' network and think tank opposed to the tyranny of corporate America and the US government and committed to the return of Vermont to its status as an independent republic, as it had been between 1777 and 1791.

18. Daily Bell: Why did you move to Vermont? Was your activism mostly as a result of the increased activity of the US military industrial complex?

During my last four years at Duke, we actually lived in Richmond, Virginia, where I commuted back to Duke weekly. Unfortunately, Richmond was going to hell in a handbasket. There were 160 homicides for 200,000 people during our last year. In a big year Vermont experiences a dozen murders for a population of 625,000 people. My wife had three personal friends independently murdered in Richmond.

The move to Vermont was motivated by a longing for community and the search for a proxy for an alpine village. Vermont is neat, clean, rural, green, democratic, nonviolent, safe, noncommercial, egalitarian, and humane. It is a mirror image of the way America once was but no longer knows how to be.

Supporters of the Second Vermont Republic would like to free themselves from a government that condones illegal wars with Afghanistan, Iraq, Libya, and Pakistan, unconditional support for the Israeli military machine, a foreign policy based on full-spectrum dominance and imperial overstretch, multitrillion-dollar budget deficits, endless Wall Street bailouts, corporate greed and fraud, environmental degradation, dependence on imported oil, and a culture of deceit.

Secession: The Second Vermont Republic

2. *Daily Bell: How did you come to be involved in the Vermont secessionist movement?*

Nearly three years before I moved to Vermont, on October 9, 1990, *The Bennington Banner* published my article entitled "Should the US Be Downsized?" Four years later in *Challenge* (November 1994), I wrote "The time has come both for the individual states and the federal government to begin planning the rational downsizing of America." Continuing, I suggested that Vermont might lead the way by helping "save our nation from the debilitating effects of big government and big business" and by "providing an independent role model for the other states to follow."

In 1997 William H. Willimon and I published *Downsizing the USA*, which not only called for Vermont independence but the peaceful dissolution of the American empire. We argued that the US government had become too big, too centralized, too powerful, too undemocratic, too militaristic, too imperialistic, too materialistic, and too unresponsive to the needs of individual citizens and small communities. However, since we were in the midst of the greatest economic boom in history, few Americans were interested in downsizing anything. The name of the game was "up, up, and away." Only bigger and faster were thought to be better.

For the most part, before September 11, 2001, my call for Vermont independence and the dissolution of the empire fell on deaf ears. It was as though I were speaking to an audience of one, namely myself. But a year or so after 9/11, that gradually began to change. On March 5, 2003, two weeks before the second war with Iraq began, I spoke at an antiwar rally at Johnson State College and decided to test-market the idea of an independent Vermont.

Basically, my pitch to the students was, "If you want to prevent future wars in places such as Afghanistan and Iraq, we have no choice but to break up the United States into smaller regions, and that process should begin with Vermont declaring its independence from the United States." They were stunned, but they got it. Their positive response literally provided the energy to launch the Second Vermont Republic.

Ten days after the bombing began in Baghdad on March 19, 2003, we held the first of four monthly meetings at the Village Cup in Jericho to discuss how such a movement might evolve. These meetings were attended by only a handful of people. Early on we decided not to become a political party but rather a civic club. The name "Second Vermont Republic" was proposed by

Jeffersonville High School student Walker Brook and registered with the Secretary of State on June 19, 2003.

Over lunch in the backyard of the Bread & Puppet Theater Museum in Glover, Vermont, on July 18, 2003, the puppeteers, under the leadership of Peter Schumann, agreed to cooperate with the Second Vermont Republic to promote Vermont independence.

In conjunction with the release of my book *The Vermont Manifesto* on October 11, 2003, the first statewide meeting of the Second Vermont Republic was held in the New Building of the Bread & Puppet Theater in Glover. The daylong meeting was attended by around fifty people.

During the two preceding years, I received a dozen or so letters from Ambassador George F. Kennan and Harvard economist John Kenneth Galbraith voicing their support for a Second Vermont Republic. About the idea of Vermont independence, Kennan said, "I see nothing fanciful, and nothing towards the realization of which the efforts of enlightened people might not be usefully directed." Galbraith added, "I must assure you of my pleasure in, and approval of, your views of the Second Vermont Republic."

3. *Daily Bell: Tell us more about the movement itself. How has it unfolded, and where it is going?*

The Second Vermont Republic is a nonviolent citizens' network and think tank committed to: (1) the peaceful breakup of meganations such as the United States, Russia, and China; (2) the political independence of breakaway states, such as Quebec, Scotland, and Vermont; and (3) a strategic alliance with other small, democratic, nonviolent, affluent, socially responsible, cooperative, egalitarian, sustainable, ecofriendly nations, such as Austria, Finland, and Switzerland, which share a high degree of environmental integrity and a strong sense of community.

Supporters of the Second Vermont Republic subscribe to the following set of principles:

1. political independence
2. human scale
3. sustainability
4. economic solidarity
5. power sharing
6. equal opportunity
7. tension reduction
8. community

Major Events

October 11, 2003—(Second Vermont Republic) holds first statewide meeting at the Bread & Puppet Theater in Glover, Vermont.

June 19, 2004—Parade in downtown Montpelier, with Bread & Puppet followed by state house rally attended by 350 people. Vermont declares independence.

November 5–7, 2004—SVR (Second Vermont Republic) and the Fourth World sponsor an international conference on "After the Fall of America, Then What?" The Middlebury Institute is launched.

January 15, 2005—SVR celebrates Vermont Independence Day at the Langdon Street Café in Montpelier.

March 4, 2005—SVR holds a memorial service to commemorate the day in 1791 when Vermont joined the Union.

April 22, 2005—Award-winning journal *Vermont Commons* is launched.

April 2005—Vermont legislature adopts resolution naming January as Vermont History and Independence month.

June 3–5, 2005—SVR officially represented at the fifteenth national Congress of the Parti Québécois in Quebec City.

October 28, 2005—SVR holds first statewide convention on secession in the US since 1861. The event takes place in the house chamber of the state house and is attended by three hundred people.

November 3–5, 2006—Middlebury Institute holds First North American Secessionist Convention in Burlington, Vermont. The convention attracts delegates from sixteen secessionist organization in eighteen states.

April 12, 2007—UVM Center for Rural Studies releases results of its annual "Vermonter Poll" showing that 13 percent of eligible voters in Vermont support secession, up from 8 percent a year earlier.

June 3, 2007—Associated Press releases a piece entitled "In Vermont, Nascent Secession Movement Gains Traction." Article is run worldwide by hundreds of newspapers, websites, radio stations, and TV stations.

June 4–5, 2007—SVR founder Thomas H. Naylor is interviewed by Fox News three separate times, including on *The O'Reilly Factor*.

October 3–4, 2007—Second North American Secessionist

Convention takes place in Chattanooga, Tennessee. Representatives from thirty states attend. It too receives worldwide media attention.

November 7, 2008—Second Statewide Convention on Vermont Independence in the house chamber of the state house in Montpelier.

November 14–16, 2008—Third North American Secession Convention in Manchester, New Hampshire.

May 22, 2009—Dennis Steele launches Radio Free Vermont, a Vermont-based music internet station.

October 6, 2009—SVR issues Scott Nearing fifty clover silver tokens.

January 15, 2010—Ten secessionists announce their candidacy for the November 2 election, including candidates for governor and lieutenant governor, seven Senate seats, and one House seat.

January 10, 2011—SVR named one of the "Top 10 Aspiring Nations" in the world by *Time* magazine.

September 14, 2012—Third Statewide Convention on Vermont Independence in the house chamber of the state house in Montpelier. Keynote speakers: Morris Berman and Lierre Keith.

Thomas Naylor's Paths to Peace: Small Is Necessary 43

Third Statewide Convention on Vermont Independence, September 14, 2012, Vermont state house.

"We are all in the same boat." Third Statewide Convention on Vermont Independence, September 14, 2012, outside the Vermont state house.

4. *Daily Bell: It is not so much in the news these days? Is it less of a force?*

Three events put SVR on the political radar screen, so to speak: (1) George W. Bush's response to 9/11—the war on terror; (2) the 2003 war in Iraq; and (3) the 2004 reelection of Bush. Bush was probably the movement's greatest asset.

Vermont is perhaps the most left-wing state in the nation. Two-thirds of the voters supported Barack Obama in his 2008 election bid. To the political left in Vermont, led by Senator Bernie Sanders, Obama represented the Second Coming of Jesus Christ. After three years, some Vermonters on the political left have finally figured out that Obama does not walk on water and is merely a smirk-free George W. Bush. But because he is smarter, more articulate, and more charismatic than Bush, he is much more dangerous. Secession is a very tough sell in Vermont as well as elsewhere. In January of 2009, it became a much tougher sell.

Abraham Lincoln really did a number on us 150 years ago. He convinced most Americans on the political right as well as the left that secession is a complete anathema. Secession is thought by most to be immoral, illegal, and unconstitutional. Never mind the Declaration of Independence, the fact that the United States was born out of secession from England, the tenth amendment to the Constitution, and the escape clauses which three of the original thirteen states had built into their respective constitutions. Secession immediately conjures up images of slavery, the Civil War, racism, and violence. Many otherwise intelligent Americans neither know how to pronounce or spell the word *secession*. More often than not it is pronounced as though the correct spelling were *s-u-c-c-e-s-s-i-o-n*.

Because of the perceived absurdity of tiny Vermont confronting the most powerful empire of all time, the Second Vermont Republic has arguably attracted more attention outside of Vermont than within. It's a classic David and Goliath.

Since its inception, SVR has employed two quite different parallel strategies in its efforts to promote secession—a hard-sell approach and a soft-sell approach. Neither has proven to be particularly effective.

The hard sell paradigm confronts the issue head on. Because of its size, the US government has become unmanageable and unfixable. Our nation has lost its moral authority and is unsustainable. A state such as Vermont either goes down with the *Titanic* or seeks other options. Secession is one such option. But because of its association with the Civil War, secession is toxic as hell. The mere mention of the word brings forth the charges of racism from the political left. It is virtually impossible to have an intelligent conversation about the subject with a liberal ideologue.

The alternative paradigm speaks of political independence as though it were some desired state of being achievable in the future only after a state such as Vermont achieves economic, energy, and agricultural independence. Middlebury College environmentalist Bill McKibben has wrongheadedly convinced many Vermonters that political independence is an impossible dream without food and energy independence. McKibben is apparently unaware of the fact that Japan, the third largest economy in the world, imports every drop of oil it consumes as well as most of its food. Secession is not a synonym for economic isolationism.

The problem with the soft-sell paradigm is that its supporters are so busy planting organic gardens, building root cellars, cutting their own wood, acquiring solar panels, and driving their Priuses that they don't even notice the nine-hundred-pound gorilla in the room, namely, the American empire. So benign is the soft-sell approach that is adherents never get around to talking about political independence.

Nine years of experience with the Second Vermont Republic have convinced me that the real issue is not Vermont, states' rights, secession, political independence, energy independence, agricultural independence, or economic independence but rather the American empire itself. In the words of economist Paul Craig Roberts, "The United States is an immoral country, with an immoral people and an immoral government. Americans no longer have a moral conscience. They have gone over to the dark side."

There is no longer any moral justification whatsoever for the existence of the United States. The only morally defensible alternative to empire is peaceful dissolution.

So long as the empire remains intact, there will be no end to all the nasty little wars, corporate personhood, Wall Street dominance, and our unconditional support for the Israeli military machine. These are all gifts from the empire.

Peaceful dissolution could be initiated at the state, regional, or national level through some combination of demonstrations, strikes, protests, tax revolts, civil disobedience, and eventually secession. The US Congress could even initiate dissolution, but don't hold your breath over that option.

Since dissolution would be nationwide in scope, it would arguably be less self-centered and less ethnocentric than if a single state such as Alaska, Texas, or Vermont tried to go it alone. Everyone has skin in the game, so to speak. The primary focus would not be on "What's in it for my state?" but rather on ending global dominance and military madness, stopping the exploitation of the poor and the middle class by the superrich, curbing the use of fossil fuels and other natural resources, curtailing the dependence on economic growth at any cost, reining in corruption and deceit, and ending the suppression of civil liberties.

Maine, New Hampshire, and Vermont, for example, might join the four Atlantic provinces of Canada to create a little country the size of Denmark and call it New Acadia. Upstate New York and New York City might split into two separate countries. Chicago and Los Angeles could become independent city-states. Alaska, Hawaii, Puerto Rico, Florida, and Texas might go it alone, with South Texas and South Florida splitting off separately. It's not hard to imagine California being divided into three countries and Washington, Oregon, and British Columbia evolving into Cascadia. A New South and a Rocky Mountain Republic also seem like likely possibilities.

We have no illusion that a large number of Americans will embrace dissolution any time soon. Our problems will have to become a lot worse before that happens. But the time to start the conversation is now! How many people predicted the 1991 implosion of the Soviet Union? Planned, orderly dissolution is surely preferable to unexpected collapse and utter chaos.

If the Tea Party and Occupy Wall Street eventually figure out that the US government is unfixable, then they may both turn to peaceful dissolution as the only game in town.

20. Daily Bell: You were involved in the 2004 "radical consultation" among various grassroots secessionist groups in Middlebury, Vermont, which resulted in the creation of the Middlebury Institute. Tell us about that.

November 5–7, 2004, forty people from eleven states and England attended a conference at the Middlebury Inn, cosponsored by SVR and the Fourth World of Wessex, England, entitled "After the Fall of America, Then What?" The Fourth World, which published *The Fourth World Review*, a periodical inspired by Leopold Kohr and Fritz Schumacher, was committed to small nations, small communities, small farms, small shops, the human scale, and the inalienable sovereignty of the human spirit. Speakers included Kirkpatrick Sale, Robert Allio, Frank Bryan, and Thomas H. Naylor.

The underlying premise of the conference was that the United States had become unsustainable, ungovernable, and unfixable. If that were indeed the case, then do we go down with the *Titanic* or seek other alternatives? Among the options discussed at Middlebury were denial, compliance, and political reform—proven to be dead ends; revolution, rebellion, and implosion—equally problematic; and decentralization, devolution, and peaceful dissolution. The conference also included a mock town meeting.

At the close of the meeting over half of the delegates signed *The Middlebury Declaration* (reprinted on p. 18ff.) which called for the creation of a movement that would "place secession on the national agenda, encourage secessionist organizations, develop communication among existing and future secessionist groups, and create a body of scholarship to examine and promote the ideas and principles of secessionism." The Middlebury Institute headed by Kirkpatrick Sale is now engaged in the pursuit of these goals. The Middlebury Institute sponsored three North American Secession Conventions in Burlington, Vermont (2006), Chattanooga, Tennessee (2007), and Manchester, New Hampshire (2008).

Intellectual Life

5. *Daily Bell: Tell us about the books you have written on secession and how you came to focus so forcefully on this issue.*

I have published three books on secession: *Downsizing the USA* (with William Willimon, 1997), *The Vermont Manifesto* (2003), and *Secession* (2008). Given the level of ignorance about secession in the United States, the degree to which it has been demonized, and the fact that there were virtually no books on the subject, I decided to take a shot at it.

6. *Daily Bell: What are you doing now? How do you make a living? Are you switching careers in a sense?*

I spend most of my time writing about Vermont independence and the peaceful dissolution of the American empire. I write for the SVR website as well as CounterPunch.

My personal income comes from my Duke retirement, book royalties, speaking fees, and investments in gold. My wife has a real job.

As my friend Yale economist Martin Shubik used to say, the Second Vermont Republic keeps me out of the pool halls.

7. *Daily Bell: It is interesting that you have degrees in science and*

industrial engineering. You also received a master's in business from Indiana University in 1961 and a doctor of philosophy in economics from Tulane University in 1964. How did you become so motivated to learn so much?

Mathematics, computers, and economic theory provide the underlying linkages connecting my academic disciplines. These tools are also useful for conceptualizing complex socioeconomic and political problems. As for motivation, if one grew up in Jackson, Mississippi, in the 1950s, one couldn't avoid being imbued with a heavy dose of the Protestant ethic and an intense desire to get out of Dodge.

8. *Daily Bell: Did you intend to become a kind of Renaissance man?*

One of the advantages of teaching at Duke University was that it afforded me the opportunity and the freedom to reinvent myself every few years. By that I mean the freedom to go into some totally unrelated field about which I knew nothing. Although I began my career as an econometric model builder in 1964, I became actively involved in southern politics in 1969 and also launched a ten-year career in corporate simulation-model building that year. SIMPLAN Systems was started in 1971. During the 1980s I did a lot of consulting for major companies in strategic planning. Beginning in 1982 and continuing until the Soviet Union imploded in 1991, the Soviet Union and Eastern Europe were my passions. Then in 1991 I turned to the search for meaning and French writer Albert Camus. Today I am at work on a philosophy of peaceful rebellion against the human condition—separation, meaninglessness, powerlessness, and death.

9. *Daily Bell: You taught at Duke, which is known as a communally oriented academy. Did you absorb this ethos?*

Clearly I benefited from the sense of community at Duke University. However, my interest in community took a quantum leap forward in 1992 while my wife and I were working on *The Search for Meaning*. We decided to take a family vacation in Switzerland, Austria, and Northern Italy to see if life in Alpine villages was all that it was cracked up to be. We wrote about this in our book and moved to Vermont in search of community.

10. *Daily Bell: Do you consider yourself a socialist? A progressive? How would you peg yourself?*

I am a left-leaning libertarian with strong anarchist tendencies. This means that I believe there are two enemies, the US government and corporate America, the latter of which owns the former.

Although I voted for Nixon in 1960, Kennedy had won me over by 1962. I remained a liberal Democrat until the early 1990s when slick Willie Clinton pushed me over the brink. In addition to being a pathological liar, Clinton was a conservative Republican disguised as a liberal Democrat. He gave the Republicans their every wish. He made me realize that there is absolutely no difference between the Democratic and Republican parties. They are both corrupt to the core.

11. *Daily Bell: You taught economics. Are you a Keynesian? An Austrian?*

I am mostly a pragmatic eclectic. Every time I was being considered for promotion (twice) at Duke, there was only one issue. "Is Naylor a real economist or not?" It was probably the right question.

Basically, I am favorably disposed toward markets. I am also a gold bug. Does that make me an Austrian? On the other hand, I am not averse to the use of government spending to stimulate the economy. Does that make me a Keynesian?

Two of my favorite economists were Joan Robinson, a Marxist, and Leopold Kohr, an Austrian.

12. *Daily Bell: Can you give us a critique of why Austrian economics has expanded so fast? Coincidence? Internet?*

I believe Ronald Reagan and Margaret Thatcher did about as much for Chicago and Austrian economics as anything else.

The Internet

13. *Daily Bell: What kind of impact has the internet had on the world and your movement?*

The Vermont independence network has no doubt benefited from the internet. We have four websites, and most of our supporters communicate via email. However, I am not nearly so sanguine about the internet as most. It may be one of the most anti-intellectual, anti-educational, anticreative, antisocial devices ever invented—capable of destroying community, undermining democracy, creating a spiritual vacuum, inducing emotional instability, and downloading the human mind.

My view of the internet is similar to Henry David Thoreau's view of the magnetic telegraph. "We are in great haste to construct a magnetic telegraph from Maine to Texas, but Maine and Texas may have nothing important to communicate. We are eager to tunnel the Atlantic and bring the Old World nearer the New, but perchance the first news that will leak through into the broad, flapping American ear will be that Princess Adelaide has the whooping cough."

Microsoft's Bill Gates and others claim that the internet leads to empowerment and enhanced democracy. But who is being empowered by whom? As e-mania has exploded, voter turnout has declined, as well as every other form of civic participation, including involvement in religious groups, town meetings, local school activities, civic clubs, union meetings, and political organizations. People transfixed by PCs and cell phones have little time to participate in anything and are a threat to no one.

If one surfs the internet, one can find hundreds, if not thousands, of Web sites espousing every conceivable political philosophy. There are endless blogs and chat rooms devoted to the discussion of politics. But is anyone really listening to all of this electronic chatter? Above all, what the Net does extremely well is keep us busy—distracted from noticing what the cipherpriests are doing to us in the name of freedom and democracy. Social networks like Facebook are more of the same.

While individual internet junkies pretend to be doing their own thing, in reality they are insignificant pawns in a vast global experiment in commercially controlled anarchy. They are, in fact, doing precisely what the high priests would have them do.

14. *Daily Bell: Is the internet a kind of modern Gutenberg Press?*

I believe I have already answered this question. I have no email address, no cell phone, and no telephone answering machine, but I do have a copy machine.

The Business World

15. *Daily Bell: You were president in the 1970s of a fifty-person computer software firm with Fortune 500 clients worldwide. You were also an international management consultant advising major corporations and governments in over thirty countries. What do you think of corporate America? Is it a problem?*

I have the same problem with corporate America that I do with the US government—size! Many American corporations, banks, and other financial institutions, just like the federal government, are simply too big. In the words of Leopold Kohr: "There seems only one cause behind all forms of social misery: *bigness*. It appears to be the one and only problem permeating all creation. Wherever something is wrong, something is too big."

16. *Daily Bell: Are modern corporations a problem? Do you think they need to be further regulated?*

Big corporations are a problem. Small ones are not.

If Vermont had been an independent republic ten years or so ago, it could have kept Walmart out. However, the US Constitution makes it virtually impossible to do so. Walmart is the Great Satan of corporate America.

I am against all forms of bigness—big government, big business, big cities, big farms, big schools, big universities, big buildings, big churches, big military, and big social welfare.

Sustainability

22. *Daily Bell: We have identified a lot of Green influences on the Vermont secession movement. Are you behind a carbon tax agenda?*

I think it is safe to say that there is a strong green influence in the Vermont independence movement. Although *Vermont Commons*, the multimedia voice of Vermont independence, has most likely published some pieces about the carbon tax, it is not one of our passions. Remember, we are more interested in dissolving the empire rather than fixing it.

29. Daily Bell: Is the Vermont secessionist movement formally Green, as the Huffington Post *suggested?*

The SVR mission statement says:

Sustainability: We celebrate and support Vermont's small, clean, green, sustainable, socially responsible towns, farms, businesses, schools, and churches. We encourage family-owned farms and businesses to produce innovative, premium-quality, healthy products. We also believe that energy independence is an essential goal toward which to strive.

30. Daily Bell: The New Hampshire secessionist movement is not Green. Is this why you have not made common cause with them?

I am assuming you are referring to the New Hampshire Free State Project. It is not a secession movement. Its primary aim seems to be to abolish the government of New Hampshire and create a state that has no government and no taxes. SVR is not in that business.

Also, a couple of years ago, I spoke at the Free State's annual convention. Half of the people there were actually carrying loaded weapons, as if to say, "Mine is bigger than yours." Vermont has no gun control laws, but you will not find people at the SVR statewide convention walking around with loaded weapons. Frankly, I thought it looked pretty stupid!

On Ron Paul

31. Daily Bell: Where do you stand on Ron Paul? Will you vote for him? Will your movement endorse him? Why or why not? Is he a friend of secessionism?

I like Ron Paul a lot. After all, he is a graduate of the Duke University Medical School, just like my wife. Ironically, I met him in 1995 at a secession conference sponsored by the Von Mises Institute in Charleston, South Carolina. It may have been the most interesting conference I ever attended.

I find myself in complete agreement with his positions on foreign policy, reduced military spending, Israel, and the Federal Reserve. But in his heart of hearts, Ron Paul seems to believe that the US government is still fixable. All we need do is return to the Constitution, and everything will be just fine. But it will never happen. Our Congress is owned, operated, and controlled by Wall Street and corporate America. They like the way the Constitution is being interpreted and will see to it that nothing changes.

In the end, Ron Paul, not unlike the Tea Party and Occupy Wall Street, is just another distraction preventing the American people from seeing that America is in a death spiral. We will not be able to reform our way out. This is the endgame! The vast majority of Americans are in a complete state of denial. Congressman Paul, the Tea Party, and Occupy Wall Street are there to make sure we don't wake up.

The American Empire, No Such Thing as a Just War

19. Daily Bell: Should the US cut back on welfare as well as the military industrial complex, or should the US aggressively provide more military aid to countries that have been apparently identified as potentially in danger of "terrorist" destabilization?

There is no such thing as a just war. Wars are about money, power, wealth, size, and greed. Wars are fought not to achieve social justice but to serve the interests of political elites pretending to be patriots, who demonize their alleged enemies so as to manipulate their minions into sacrificing their lives for false ideals.

The threat of Islamic terrorism is a problem of our government's own making. It is grounded in American arrogance, ignorance, racism, imperialism, and support for the terrorist state of Israel. President Bush's so-called war on terror was an insidious campaign to create fear and hatred among Americans and Europeans toward Muslims so as to rationalize a foreign policy aimed at doing whatever is necessary to control their oil in the Middle East. Under President Obama it's more of the same. Plus, the threat of terrorism helps justify trillion-dollar-plus defense budgets, 1.6 million American troops stationed in one thousand bases in over 153 countries, special operations strike forces in 120 countries, and pilotless drone aircraft operating worldwide.

32. Daily Bell: Where do you stand generally on the US as empire? Ron Paul disagrees with this sort of Leviathan.

A nation that has nearly one thousand military bases in 153 countries, by definition, cannot be anything other than an empire.

President Obama's 2012 "Proud to be an American" State of the Union address was little more than a collection of narcissistic American clichés aggrandizing our military prowess and hyping war with Iran. Among the Republican candidates for president, only Ron Paul has not engaged in this form of demagogic drivel.

As today's most warlike nation, America's penchant for trying to solve complex geopolitical problems with simplistically violent and destructive military solutions goes virtually unchallenged.

Unfortunately, there is absolutely nothing new about the notion of American exceptionalism. Its historical origins can be traced back to the concept of "manifest destiny" or "God's will" to justify our annihilation of Native Americans starting in the sixteenth century. Although our nation was founded on the principles of life, liberty, and the pursuit of happiness, the story of how Native Americans were relentlessly forced to abandon their homes and lands and move into Indian territories to make room for American states is one of arrogance, greed, and raw military power.

The barbaric conquest of Native Americans continued for several hundred years and involved many of our most cherished national heroes, including George Washington, Thomas Jefferson, James Monroe, and Andrew Jackson, to mention only a few. Adding insult to injury, the US government has violated over three hundred treaties that were signed to protect the rights of the American Indians.

In over two hundred years, the North American continent has never been attacked—nor even seriously threatened with invasion by Japan, Germany, the Soviet Union, or anyone else. Despite this fact, over a million Americans have been killed in wars and trillions of dollars have been spent by the military—$13 trillion on the Cold War alone.

Far from defending its homeland, Washington has drafted citizens to die in the battlefields of Europe (twice), on tropical Pacific islands, and in the jungles of Southeast Asia. On dozens of occasions political leaders have used minor incidents as provocation to justify sending troops to such far-flung places as China, Russia, Egypt, Greenland, Uruguay, the Samoa Islands, Cuba, Mexico, Haiti, Nicaragua, Panama, Grenada, Lebanon, and Iraq. Today the United States has a military presence in 153 countries.

Back in the 1980s, even as it was accusing the Soviet Union of excessive military aggression, the Reagan administration was participating in nine known wars—Afghanistan, Angola, Cambodia, Chad, El Salvador, Ethiopia, Lebanon, Morocco, and Nicaragua. The US bombed Tripoli after the CIA alleged that Libyan secret forces blew up a nightclub in West Berlin, invaded Grenada, and repeatedly attempted to remove Panamanian dictator Manuel Noriega.

President Bush I deployed over a half million American troops, fifty warships, and over one thousand warplanes to the Persian Gulf in 1991 at the "invitation of King Fahd of Saudi Arabia to teach Saddam Hussein a lesson." Most Americans proudly supported this little war. President Clinton's repeated bombing of Iraq invoked a similar response, even though the Iraqi people had never inflicted any harm on the United States. It matters not whether we send troops to Haiti, Somalia, Bosnia, or Kosovo or bomb Afghanistan, Pakistan, or Libya. America is "exceptional." We're number one, and might makes right.

And since 9/11, the Bush-Obama war on terror has just been more of the same. Full-spectrum dominance and imperial overstretch are the premises on which American foreign policy is based. All of which leads to so-called smart diplomacy that means sending in drones, Navy SEALs, and Delta Force death squads to show who's boss. That's what American exceptionalism is all about—empire!

37. Daily Bell: Are you worried about growing authoritarianism in the US?

Yes. Virtually everything we ever accused the Soviets of back in the 1980s we are guilty of in spades. Ronald Reagan was right when he accused the Soviet Union of being an evil empire. What he overlooked was the fact that it was not the only evil empire in the world.

Smaller Is Better, the Role of Government

33. Daily Bell: You don't think the US is governable anymore. Do you believe in smaller government?

Just as it was impossible to manage 280 million people from one central bureau in Moscow, so too is it impossible to manage 310 million people from Washington. The Soviet Union was too big and contained too many heterogeneous republics, ethnic minorities, religions, and nationalities to be run by Kremlin bureaucrats. Why should we be surprised that gridlock is the rule on Capitol Hill? What else could we expect from one legislative body trying to represent so many heterogeneous states, ethnic minorities, political ideologies, and religious sects? The United States is ungovernable and, therefore, unfixable. It is but one of eleven countries in the world that has a population of over one hundred million people, all of which are ungovernable.

I believe the time has come for the smaller nations of the world to confront the meganations and say, "Enough is enough. We refuse to continue condoning your plundering the planet in pursuit of resources and markets to quench your insatiable appetite for consumer goods and services." These small nations should call for the nonviolent breakup of the United States, China, Russia, India, Japan, and the other meganations of the world.

A small group of peaceful, sustainable, cooperative, democratic, egalitarian, ecofriendly nations might lead the way. Such a group might include Denmark, Finland, Norway, Sweden, and Switzerland.

What these five European nations have in common is that they are tiny, very affluent, nonviolent, democratic, and socially responsible. They also have a high degree of environmental integrity and a strong sense of community. Although Denmark and Norway are members of NATO, Finland, Sweden, and Switzerland are neutral. Once considered classical European democratic socialist states, the four Nordic states in the group have become much more market-oriented in recent years. Not only is Switzerland the wealthiest of the lot, but it is the most market-oriented country in the world, with the weakest central government, the most decentralized social welfare system, and a long tradition of direct democracy. What's more, all these countries work, and they work very well. Compared to the United States they have fewer big cities, less traffic congestion, less pollution, less poverty, less crime, less drug abuse, and fewer social welfare problems.

Three other small countries that might also join the party are environmentally friendly Costa Rica, which has no army; ecovillages pioneer Senegal; and the Himalayan kingdom of Bhutan. Since 1982 the king of Bhutan has been trying to make gross national happiness the national priority rather than gross national product. Although still a work in progress, policies instituted by the king are aimed at ensuring that prosperity is shared across society and that it is balanced against preserving cultural traditions, protecting the environment, and maintaining a responsive government.

This group of small, nonviolent, sustainable countries could evolve into the Small Nations' Alliance. Such an alliance might encourage the nonviolent breakup of meganations, the peaceful coexistence of a community of like-minded, small nations, and the independence of small breakaway states such as Quebec, Tibet, and Vermont from larger nations. The Small Nations' Alliance could become a sort of international cheerleader supporting breakaway nations.

We do not envision the SNA as an international governing body with the power to impose its collective will on others. Rather we see it as a role model encouraging others to decentralize, downsize, localize, demilitarize, simplify, and humanize their lives. Membership in the SNA will be open to those nations who subscribe to the principles of the SNA and are approved for membership by a consensus of SNA members. The only mechanism available for enforcing policies endorsed by the SNA would be expulsion from the organization for noncompliance.

According to Leopold Kohr: "A small-state world would not only solve the problems of social brutality and war; it would solve the problems of oppression and tyranny. It would solve all problems arising from power."

34. Daily Bell: What should government do?

Power Sharing. Vermont's strong democratic tradition is grounded in its town meetings. We favor devolution of political power from the state back to local communities, making the governing structure for towns, schools, hospitals, and social services much like that of Switzerland. Shared power also underlies our approach to international relations.

Equal Opportunity. We support equal access for all Vermont citizens to quality education, housing, employment, and health care.

Tension Reduction. Consistent with Vermont's long tradition of "live and let live" and nonviolence, we do not condone any form of state-sponsored violence. An independent Vermont will have no standing army. In its place will be a voluntary citizens' brigade to reduce tension and restore order in the event of civil unrest and to provide assistance when natural disasters occur. Tension reduction is the bedrock principle on which all international conflicts are to be resolved.

Community. We support a strong sense of community among our citizens and their neighbors, including their international neighbors.

Four Steps to the Future

36. Daily Bell: What is the future of your movement and the US secessionist movement in general?

Secession is a radical form of rebellion grounded in anger and fear with a positive vision of the future. For reasons stated previously, secession is a very tough sell in Vermont and elsewhere.

The decision to secede necessarily involves a very personal, painful four-step process:

1. *Denunciation.* The United States has lost its moral authority and is unsustainable, ungovernable, and unfixable.

2. *Disengagement.* I don't want to go down with the *Titanic*.
3. *Demystification.* Secession is a viable option constitutionally, politically, and economically.
4. *Defiance.* I personally want to help take my state back from big business, big markets, and big government, and I want to do so peacefully.

By far the most difficult step in the process of deciding to embrace secession is the emotional one of letting go of one's images of America as "the home of the free and the brave" and "the greatest nation in the world." These images have been ingrained in most of us since early childhood. Reinforced by World War II, the Cold War, and an uncritical education system, and our pro-American media, they are very difficult and painful to shake.

The decision to secede involves reaching the point where you are unwilling to risk going down with the *Titanic* and must seek out other options while there are still other options on the table. Secession is one such option. But it may very well be the only viable option available to us.

The Second Vermont Republic has neither the resources nor the persuasive powers to convince people to consider secession. Unfortunately, our problems will have to become much worse before a significant number of people will become more interested in secession in Vermont or elsewhere. However, some combination of the collapse of the euro, the war with Iran, or the election of Mitt Romney could give rise to a dramatic increase in interest in secession.

Our next major event will take place in the house chamber of the Vermont state house in Montpelier on September 14, 2012 It will be our third statewide convention on Vermont independence. Keynote speakers will be Morris Berman, author of *Why America Failed*, and Lierre Keith, coauthor of *Deep Green Resistance.*

The Principality of Liechtenstein: A Model of Self-Determination for a World Filled with Chaos

Thomas Naylor

Why should a tiny alpine nation nestled between the Swiss and Austrian Alps with a population of only thirty-five thousand spread over 62 square miles, no airport, one hospital, 155 miles of paved roadway, and only irregular local train service be taken seriously by anyone? Because it has the highest gross domestic product per person in the world when adjusted by purchasing power parity (over $140,000 per capita), the world's lowest external debt, and the second lowest unemployment rate in the world (recently as low as 1.5 percent). But the Principality of Liechtenstein happens to be just such a place.

Liechtenstein is a constitutional monarchy organized as a unitary parliamentary democracy with an enlightened reigning prince by the name of Hans-Adam II. Since the constitutional reform of 2003 was implemented by the prince, the citizens of Liechtenstein actually have the right to abolish the monarchy altogether. Hans-Adam has a quite unique philosophy of government for a reigning monarch. In his view citizens should not be seen as servants of the state, but rather as customers of a benevolent service company, otherwise known as the state, whose aim is to serve its customers. If the customers don't like the service, they can replace the service company, namely, the monarchy. "Ask not what a citizen can do for the state, but rather what the state can do better for the citizen than any other organization," says the prince.

Under the leadership of Hans-Adam, Liechtenstein acceded to the United Nations in 1990 and the European Economic Area in 1995. It is a member of neither the European Union nor NATO.

Even though Liechtenstein remained neutral during both world wars, it was practically an economic basket case after World War II. Much of the credit for turning it around economically lies with the prince. Liechtenstein is best known for its financial sector, which is a tax haven and home to 73,700 corporations worldwide. It has sixteen banks. However, its high-quality, high-tech industrial sector, which manufactures a variety of products including machine tools and precision instruments, accounts for 36 percent of the GDP.

The prince of Liechtenstein is not paid for his duties as head of state by either the state or the taxpayers. Unlike most other monarchies, the total cost of the Liechtenstein monarchy is covered by either the prince's or the so-called Princely House's private funds. The country's LGT Bank, for example, is owned by the royal family. The prince's personal fortune is thought to be in excess of $5 billion.

Not unlike Switzerland, Liechtenstein bankers have not escaped criticism from Wall Street and European bankers, the EU, and the US Congress for the use of secret bank accounts that can be used to evade foreign taxes, dodge creditors, and defy court orders. In February 2008 the LGT Bank was implicated in a tax-fraud scandal in Germany that strained the monarchy's relationship with the German government. International bankers don't like the fact that Swiss and Liechtenstein bankers don't always play by their rules.

In an attempt to clean up its image abroad, Liechtenstein has signed a number of treaties related to money laundering and fraud with the United States and the European Union, including the Tax Information Exchange Agreement with the US and the Anti-Fraud Agreement with the EU. On June 27, 2012, Liechtenstein and the US signed an Agreement on Exchange Cooperation in Preventing and Combating Serious Crime.

Prince Hans-Adam has always maintained a strong interest in the right to self-determination, so much so that in 2000 he founded the Liechtenstein Institute on Self-Determination at Princeton University. The Institute supports teaching, research, and publication about issues related to and emerging from self-determination, especially pertaining to the state, self-governance, sovereignty, security, and boundaries with particular consideration of sociocultural, ethnic, and religious issues involving state and nonstate actors.

On August 15, 2004, Prince Hans-Adam II appointed his elder son, Hereditary Prince Alois, his permanent deputy, in preparation for his succession to the throne. He now devotes more of his time to managing the assets of the Princely House, writing, and participating in international projects.

In 2009 Prince Hans-Adam II published an extremely interesting book, *The State in the Third Millennium* spelling out his unique and personal vision of the state at the beginning of the twenty-first century as well as strategies by which it might be achieved. His perspective as the reigning head of state of a monarchy that is also an oligarchy and a democracy, a direct democracy, is truly remarkable.

Although I do not agree with all the prince's ideas, and indeed strongly disagree with some of them, I find most of them to be quite insightful. Unlike myself, Hans-Adam is very libertarian, very free-market oriented, and very Roman Catholic, but he is very smart.

His understanding of geopolitics and global economics is highly sophisticated, not to mention his psychological sophistication as well. He seems to know exactly who he is and what it means to be the reigning monarch of a tiny European country. His lack of hubris is indeed refreshing.

As a card-carrying libertarian, there are no big surprises in the prince's portfolio of economic policy prescriptions for his third millennium state. Essentially what he has in mind is a libertarian state, if that is not an oxymoron. He calls for the privatization of social welfare, the elimination of government subsidies, an educational voucher system, a value-added tax, little or no national debt, private ownership of mineral rights, and a sophisticated precious-metal-based currency.

Since the constitutional reform of 2003, the principality's eleven municipalities have all had the right of self-determination. The prince correctly points out that the fifteen former republics of the Soviet Union also theoretically possessed that right, even though it was never exercised.

Hans-Adam's book concludes with a draft constitution for a prototype third millennium state whether it be a monarchy (kingdom X) or a republic (republic Y). Although I have never been a great fan of monarchies, the thought has passed through my mind, "Is the difference between a republic and a monarchy as great as we try to make it appear to be?" Maybe. Maybe not.

The opening of the Liechtenstein Embassy in Washington, DC, in 2002 is but one example of how Hans-Adam has attempted to foster closer ties with the United States. The embassy website contains numerous photographs of Washington dignitaries such as the Obamas and Hillary Clinton appearing at the embassy. In a 2010 interview, Hans-Adam is reported to have said, "The Americans saved us during World War II and during the Cold War." But does that, therefore, mean that Liechtenstein owes its soul to them? Apparently so.

But in a surprising turn of events for a country that disbanded its military in 1868 for financial reasons and is ruled by a live-and-let-live libertarian committed to the right of self-determination, Hans-Adam embraces the notion of the United States serving as the world's global policeman. That is, if a particular country such as Iraq, Libya, North Korea, or Syria has an authoritarian regime that is not playing by the rules set forth by the United Sates, the United States would have the right to intervene in that country, forcing it to agree to the establishment of a functioning democratic state. Although the prince gives high marks to the United States for its 2003 invasion of Iraq, he would have the United States partner with the EU to rebuild a rogue state brought down by the empire by establishing a functioning democratic constitutional state to replace the original one.

But isn't this tantamount to getting in bed with the American empire and supporting its imperialist foreign policy that is based on the concepts of full-spectrum dominance, imperial overstretch, and might makes right? Would the prince also endorse attacks by drones, Navy SEALs, and Delta Force Death Squads aimed at those unfortunate enough to find themselves on the White House kill list? All of this from an enlightened, well-educated monarch who is a staunch defender of the right of self-determination. How can this be?

Of what is the prince so afraid? Who would ever invade Liechtenstein? If so, what would they do with it?

Prince Hans-Adam II is uniquely qualified and extremely well positioned to be the foremost advocate for self-determination worldwide. Indeed, the small nations of the world such as Bhutan, Costa Rica, Denmark, Finland, Iceland, Norway, Senegal, Sweden, and Switzerland and the aspiring nations of the world such as the Basque Country, Kurdistan, Quebec, Scotland, South Ossetia, Tibet, Vermont, and Western Sahara desperately need his support to enable them to stand up to meganations such as the United States, China, Russia, India, Japan, and Brazil.

With admiration and respect, I urge him to reconsider his position. The future of the planet is at stake.

August 13, 2012

A Community of Small Nations for a Sustainable Planet

Thomas Naylor

There seems only one cause behind all forms of social misery: bigness. Whenever something is wrong, something is too big.
—*Leopold Kohr, The Breakdown of Nations*

Its $5.4-trillion economy, state-of-the-art technology, or military-like efficiency could not protect Japan from the catastrophic consequences of the March 11, 2011, earthquake, tsunami, and nuclear disaster. To be quite blunt, when you cram 127 million people onto one large island and a group of smaller ones, all prone to earthquakes, you have few degrees of freedom when disaster strikes. It's all about human scale.

Japan is but one of eleven meganations with a population of over one hundred million people. Although none of them are as wealthy, materialistic, racist, militaristic, violent, or imperialistic as the United States, all eleven of them are too big, too powerful, too undemocratic, too environmentally irresponsible, too intrusive, too insular, and too unresponsive to the needs of individual citizens and small local communities.

Thus it is hardly surprising that the 192-member United Nations, which is dominated by the United States, Russia, and China, each of which has veto power in the Security Council, has been so ineffective since its inception in 1945. Nothing illustrates this better than the UN-sponsored conferences on climate change in Kyoto in 1997 and Copenhagen in 2009. Trying to come up with solutions to a problem as complex as climate change by assembling 178 heads of state, as was the case in Kyoto, or 193 in Copenhagen, is truly an exercise in futility. The product of the twelve-day Copenhagen conference was a nonbinding agreement in which no one was committed to anything. The so-called Copenhagen agreement was a complete sham. The process was replicated in Cancun, Mexico, in 2010 with similar results.

The track record of big international governing organizations, such as the League of Nations or the United Nations, is singularly unimpressive. How many wars has the UN prevented? Certainly none in Korea, Vietnam, Cambodia, Iraq, Yugoslavia, Afghanistan, Palestine, or Africa. Global political problems are too complex for an assembly of two hundred international political leaders to sort out in a public forum. This is even more true if China and the United States refuse to budge from their positions of national self-interest. Some have cynically suggested that the UN is little more than an extension of the US State Department.

I believe it is high time for the smaller nations of the world to begin withdrawing from the United Nations. The UN is morally, intellectually, and politically bankrupt. It is time for these smaller nations to confront the meganations of the world and say, "Enough is enough. We refuse to continue condoning your plundering the planet in pursuit of resources and markets to quench your insatiable appetite for consumer goods and services." These small nations should call for the nonviolent breakup of the United States, China, Russia, India, Japan, and the other meganations of the world.

A small group of peaceful, sustainable, cooperative, democratic, egalitarian, ecofriendly nations might lead the way. Such a group might include Denmark, Finland, Norway, Sweden, and Switzerland.

What these five European nations have in common is that they are tiny, very affluent, nonviolent, democratic, and socially responsible. They also have a high degree of environmental integrity and a strong sense of community. Although Denmark and Norway are members of NATO, Finland, Sweden, and Switzerland are neutral. Once considered classical European democratic socialist states, the four Nordic states in the group have become much more market-oriented in recent years. Not only is Switzerland the wealthiest of the lot, but it is the most market-oriented country in the world, with the weakest central government, the most decentralized social welfare system, and a long tradition of direct democracy. What's more, all these countries work, and they work very well. Compared to the United States, they have fewer big cities, less traffic congestion, less pollution, less poverty, less crime, less drug abuse, and fewer social welfare problems.

Three other small countries that might also join the party are environmentally friendly Costa Rica, which has no army; ecovillage pioneer Senegal; and the Himalayan kingdom of Bhutan. Since 1972 the king of Bhutan has been trying to make gross national happiness the national priority rather than gross national product. Although still a work in progress, policies instituted by the king are aimed at ensuring that prosperity is shared across society and that it is balanced against preserving cultural traditions, protecting the environment, and maintaining a responsive government.

This group of small, nonviolent, sustainable countries could evolve into the Small Nations' Alliance. Such an alliance might encourage the nonviolent breakup of meganations, the peaceful coexistence of a community of like-minded small nations, and the independence of small breakaway states such as Quebec, Tibet, and Vermont from larger nations. The Small Nations' Alliance could become a sort of international cheerleader supporting breakaway nations.

We do not envision the SNA as an international governing body with the power to impose its collective will on others. Rather we see it as a role model encouraging others to decentralize, downsize, localize, demilitarize, simplify, and humanize their lives. Membership in the SNA will be open to those nations who subscribe to the principles of the SNA and are approved for membership by a consensus of SNA members. The only mechanism available for enforcing policies endorsed by the SNA would be expulsion from the organization for noncompliance.

Membership would be open to both free-market oriented countries as well as democratic socialist countries. For example, Cuba and Venezuela might both be possible candidates for membership, provided they become more democratic. Cuba would also need to clean up its human rights act.

The point of all of this was succinctly summarized back in 1957 by Leopold Kohr in his prescient book *The Breakdown of Nations*.

"A small-state world would not only solve the problems of social brutality and war; it would solve the problems of oppression and tyranny. It would solve all problems arising from power."

March 18, 2011

Self-Determination for Small Nations

Thomas Naylor

Editor's Note: This is an excerpt from the longer document, "Radical Small Nation Self-Determination in a Chaotic Meganation World." This excerpt explains the five aspects of self-determination. For other thoughts about the role of small nations, see, for example, pages 60 and 73.

Self-determination is an act of separation or withdrawal from a larger body.

1. Personal. Throughout life we experience an endless series of acts of self-determination, including birth, death, divorce, graduation, changing jobs, leaving home, ending a relationship, and moving to another place. Some are good; others not so good.

2. Political. It is political acts of self-determination about which people seem to become so agitated, whenever a subunit of a city, state, or nation separates from the larger body. Few Americans seem to recall that the United States was created by an act of self-determination by thirteen English colonies that separated from the British Empire. Although the self-determination of the eleven Confederate States of America precipitated a bloody civil war, self-determination need not be violent, as was the case when the Soviet Union's six Eastern European allies rid themselves of their Communist regimes in 1989. Communism was brought down peacefully in five of the six Eastern European satellites of the USSR. Not only did the US government support these acts of self-determination but it actively participated in most of them. The peaceable breakup of the Soviet Union in 1991 was more of the same. Washington has also supported independence for Kosovo, East Timor, and Taiwan.

On the other hand, the White House remains cool to the Québec separatist movement and Puerto Rican independence. It does not even acknowledge the existence of the thirty or so state independence movements within the United States. The degree of support expressed by the US government for political independence varies inversely with the distance from Washington of the independence-seeking country.

3. The Human Condition. In the case of the United States, from the standpoint of the human condition, self-determination is about confronting rather than denying, escaping from, or acquiescing to the nihilism, power, separation, violence, and death associated with the American empire. Self-determination is not for the faint of heart.

4. Maslow's Hierarchy of Needs. Some have suggested that one's inclination toward self-determination depends on the extent to which his or her needs are being met by the existing arrangement, whether it be a village, town, or state. Psychologist Abraham H. Maslow's five hierarchical categories of human needs may provide a useful paradigm for thinking about this issue:

(1) physiological requirements (food, water, and shelter)

(2) safety (economic security and protection from injury and disease)

(3) social acceptance (love, a sense of belonging, and membership in a group)

(4) self-esteem (prestige, power, and recognition)

(5) self-actualization (confidence, competence, and achievement)

In a nutshell, if your needs are not being satisfied, self-determination may be an option worthy of serious consideration.

5. A Form of Loss. So obsessed with bigness are most Americans that they view political self-determination as a form of loss or an example of complete failure. To better understand how many Americans experience the sense of loss associated with political separatism, it may be instructive to examine the five states of grief outlined in Elisabeth Kübler-Ross's 1969 book entitled *On Death and Dying*. These stages include denial, anger, bargaining, depression, and acceptance.

So imbued with the notion of American exceptionalism are American patriots that they cannot even conceive of the logical possibility of a state wanting to leave the Union. Since the American Civil War ended in 1865, the prevailing view on political self-determination of our government, the Congress, the academy, our political leaders, and the clergy has been one of complete denial. Academics, religious leaders, and lawyers won't even come close to the subject. They avoid it like the plague.

Others simply become enraged at the mere mention of the idea. Separatists are viewed as unpatriotic and disloyal. Some acknowledge the possibility of political self-determination, but "not in my lifetime." To them consideration of articles of political independence would be like entering into a pact with the devil.

After experiencing denial and anger over the thought of political self-determination, some people lapse into a state of complete depression. Finally, there are some whose defeatism takes the form of reluctant acceptance: "If you can't beat them, join them."

The point of all of this is that the decision to leave the Union is a complex psychodynamic process—a process that may trigger the release of intense negative feelings. Political self-determination is a very tough sell in the United States and elsewhere.

October 11, 2012

The Case for the Self-Determination of an American State

Thomas Naylor

1. If a state is to remain true to itself, it has no other choice than to maintain its commitment to the humanity of its citizens.

2. It must resist being subsumed by an undemocratic, materialistic, racist, militaristic, megalomanic, robotic, imperialist, technofascist, global empire.

3. The US government has lost its moral authority. It is owned, operated, and controlled by corporate America and Wall Street. It has no soul.

4. America has become unsustainable economically, politically, militarily, socially, culturally, and environmentally. It is ungovernable and, therefore, unfixable. The endgame is near.

5. It has become the largest, most powerful, most materialistic, most environmentally destructive, most racist, most militaristic, most violent empire of all time.

6. The American empire has a five-hundred-year history of racism. It was built on the backs of black slaves imported from Africa on land stolen from the Indians. Five hundred years later, our racist treatment of Indians continues unabated.

7. Under the guise of the doctrine of manifest destiny, our gov-

ernment is engaged in a highly racist War on Terror against all Muslims, a war based on the policy of full-spectrum dominance.

8. The US government provides unconditional support for the racist, apartheid, terrorist state of Israel to enable it to carry out its policy of ethnic cleansing and genocide against the Palestinians.

9. America was supposed to have been immortal, but in the end it cannot deliver.

10. Do we go down with the *Titanic*, or do we seek other alternatives while there are other options on the table?

11. "Whenever any form of government becomes destructive, it is the right of the people to alter or abolish it, and institute a new government," said Thomas Jefferson in the Declaration of Independence.

12. Just as a group has a right to form, so too does it have a right to subdivide itself, or to withdraw from a larger unit.

13. It's time peacefully to rebel against the money, power, speed, greed, size, and tyranny of corporate America, Wall Street, and the US government.

14. Nonviolence is a proactive approach to conflict resolution that goes straight to the heart and soul of power relationships and demands strength, courage, and discipline, not idle pacifism.

15. Fundamental to what it means to be an American is the right of self-determination. The time has come to free ourselves from the American empire—(1) to regain control of our lives from

big government, big business, big cities, big schools, and big computer networks; (2) to relearn how to take care of ourselves by decentralizing, downsizing, localizing, demilitarizing, simplifying, and humanizing our lives; and (3) to learn how to help others take care of themselves.

16. Self-determination is a radical act of nonviolent rebellion grounded in anger and fear tempered by a positive vision of the future that involves denunciation, disengagement, demystification, and defiance.

17. Although self-determination is completely justifiable morally, legally, and constitutionally, ultimately it is a question of political will—the political will of the withdrawing state versus the political will of the empire.

18. Radical nonviolence can undermine power and authority by withdrawing the approval, moral support, and cooperation of those who have been dealt an injustice. It derives its strength from the energy buildup and very real power of powerlessness.

19. Rebellion provides us with the faith to create meaning out of meaninglessness, the energy to connect with those from whom we are separated, the power to surmount powerlessness, and the courage to confront death.

20. When all is said and done, there is but one morally defensible option for the empire—peaceful dissolution.

October 13, 2012

Untied States of America

Thomas Naylor

Editor's Note: Naylor proposed breaking the United States into twenty smaller nations. As an exercise, why break the United States up in this way? What's the rationale for these divisions? What's the internal cohesion for each proposed state? Note what Naylor says about regional cultures in Switzerland (p. 89).

---

1. *New Acadia*—Maine, New Hampshire, and Vermont (and possibly four Atlantic provinces of Canada)
2. *New England*—Connecticut, Massachusetts, and Rhode Island
3. *Upstate New York*
4. *New York City*
5. *Pennsylvania Republic*—Delaware, New Jersey, and Pennsylvania
6. *New Republic*—District of Columbia, Maryland, and Virginia
7. *New South*—Alabama, Arkansas, Georgia, Kentucky, Louisiana, Mississippi, North Carolina, South Carolina, Tennessee, and West Virginia
8. *Florida*—(possibly South Florida as a separate republic)
9. *Texas*—(possibly South Texas as a separate republic)

10. *Midwest*—Kansas, Missouri, and Oklahoma
11. *Upper Midwest*—Illinois, Iowa, Minnesota, and Wisconsin
12. *Chicago*—Cook County
13. *Middle America*—Indiana, Michigan, and Ohio
14. *Great Plains*—Nebraska, North Dakota, and South Dakota
15. *Rocky Mountain Republic*—Arizona, Colorado, Idaho, Montana, Nevada, New Mexico, Utah, and Wyoming
16. *California*
17. *Los Angeles*—Los Angeles County
18. *Cascadia*—Oregon and Washington (and possibly British Columbia)
19. *Alaska*
20. *Hawaii*

Swiss-Like Direct Democracy in America

Thomas Naylor

Taking note of the unsustainable, unfixable, gridlock nature of the US government and its inability to fix the American economy, Gerald Celente[6] has proposed that the United States turn to Swiss-style direct democracy as an alternative way to resolve such divisive issues as the wars in Afghanistan and Iraq, the magnitude of the government's budget deficit, how to finance health care, the size of the defense budget, and national immigration policy. He envisions this being carried out on the internet.

With a population of only 7.3 million people, a little larger than that of an average American state, Switzerland is one of the wealthiest, most democratic, least violent, most market-oriented countries in the world, with the weakest central government and the most decentralized social welfare system. Founded in 1291 near Lake Lucerne, the Swiss Confederation may be the most sustainable nation-state of all time.

Situated in the heart of Europe, Switzerland has always existed in a state of tension between opening and closing its borders to the outside world. Even today it has nearly one million so-called

---

6 Gerald Celente is director of the Trends Research Institute (https://trendsresearch.com). In this short video, *Direct Democracy for US, where 21% of Adults Read Below 5th Grade Level*, he talks about direct democracy: https://www.youtube.com/watch?v=LrtNmfIVXEg.

guest workers. For centuries it has been an area of settlement and a transit region of European north-south commerce. The country's economy has long been geared to processing imported raw materials and reexporting them as finished goods, such as specialty foods and pharmaceutical products.

The Swiss enjoy state-of-the-art technology, and their banks and financial institutions are among the most stable and financially secure anywhere in the world. The same is true of the Swiss franc.

Over the past seven hundred years or so, Switzerland has developed a unique social and political structure, with a strong emphasis on federalism and direct democracy, which brings together its twenty-six cantons (tiny states), with populations ranging from 14,900 to 1,187,000, and its four languages and cultures—German, French, Italian, and Romansch. The Swiss cantons enjoy considerably more autonomy than do American states. One finds a host of local and regional cultures and traditions melded into a patchwork of sights and events that are considered "typically Swiss."

Switzerland has a coalition government with a rotating presidency in which the president serves for only one year. Many Swiss do not know who of the seven Federal Councillors in the government is the president at any given time since he or she is first among equals.

In Switzerland a petition signed by one hundred thousand voters can force a nationwide vote on a proposed constitutional change, and the signatures of only fifty thousand voters can force a national referendum on any federal law passed by Parliament.

Among the high-profile issues that have been resolved by

Swiss national referendums are women's voting rights, abortion rights, creation of a new canton, abolition of the army, and Swiss membership in the League of Nations, United Nations, World Bank, IMF, and the European Union.

Several cantons still follow the centuries-old traditions of *Landsgemeinde*, or open-air parliaments, each spring. Others are experimenting with voting over the internet.

However, it is at the commune level that Swiss democracy is most direct. Within the cantons, there are 2,902 communes in the Swiss Confederation, each run by a local authority. Just as the cantons enjoy a high degree of independence from the national government, within the cantons many of the communes also enjoy a high degree of independent authority and decision-making.

Most political scientists agree that the Swiss have taken the concept of democracy to levels heretofore unattainable any place else in the world. In his excellent book, *Direct Democracy in Switzerland* (Transaction Publishers, 2002), Gregory a Fossedal describes Switzerland as "a direct democracy, in which, to an extent, the people pass their own laws, judge the constitutionality of statutes, and even have written, in effect, their own constitution." That's a lot!

All of this is in stark contrast to the United States, in which our government is owned, operated, and controlled by Wall Street, corporate America, the Pentagon, and the Israeli government lobby. Whereas the primary role of Swiss direct democracy is to protect the Swiss people from the Swiss government, the US government is more concerned with protecting its powerful clients from the will of the American people. In Switzerland, the people own their government. In the United States, the government owns us.

But a word of caution is in order before embracing the Swiss model of direct democracy. The United States is more than forty times larger than Switzerland in terms of population. On the one hand, it has one of the most centralized governments in the world. On the other hand, it is also highly decentralized across fifty states, some of which—like California, Texas, New York, and Florida—are quite large and powerful, unlike Swiss cantons. Even if one sorts out all the conceptual, constitutional, and legal problems required to make direct democracy work in the United States, the political balancing act will be formidable.

Direct democracy works in Switzerland because Switzerland is a tiny, well-educated, hard-working country with a strong sense of community. The United States is not Switzerland.

For starters, retrofitting the US Constitution and legal system to accommodate direct democracy would require the expertise of a plethora of constitutional scholars and legal experts. Whether those legal scholars and political scientists would be up to the challenge of designing such a complex system remains to be seen.

A process would also have to be developed to bring important issues to the table for consideration by a nationwide referendum. And then there is the matter of the computer network and software required to make internet voting work.

Although introducing direct democracy into the United States sounds like a very good idea, it would involve a number of conceptual, legal, constitutional, economic, technical, and political challenges. Such a move would require bold, creative political leadership combined with world-class marketing skills.

But the alternative is a nation whose government has lost its moral authority and is tightly controlled by a self-serving military-industrial-congressional complex accountable only to itself—a nation that has become unsustainable economically, militarily, socially, environmentally, and politically. The United States is so large that it may no longer be governable and has possibly become unfixable.

If there is a way out of our nation's death spiral, direct democracy just might be one of our last remaining viable options. We could do a lot worse than emulating the Swiss.

Secession Fever Spreads Globally

Thomas Naylor

Editor's Note: One of Naylor's last pieces, perhaps *the* last.

We should devote our efforts to the creation of numerous small principalities throughout the world, where people can live in happiness and freedom. The large states... must be convinced of the need to decentralize politically in order to bring democracy and self-determination into the smallest political units, namely local communities, be they villages or cities.

—Hans-Adam II, Prince of Liechtenstein,
The State in the Third Millennium

Since the reelection of Barack Obama on November 6, over one million Americans have signed petitions on a White House website known as "We the People" calling for the secession of their respective states from the Union. Contrary to the view expressed by many politically correct liberals, this is not merely a knee-jerk, racist reaction of some Tea Party types to the reelection of Obama, but rather it is part of a well-defined trend. Today there are, in fact, 250 self-determined political independence movements in play worldwide, including nearly 100 in Europe alone, over 70 in Asia, 40 in Africa, 30 or so in North America, and 15 to 20 scattered on various islands around the world. We could be on the brink of a global secession pandemic!

We live in a meganation world under the cloud of an empire, the American empire. Fifty-nine percent of the people on the planet now live in one of the eleven nations with a population of over one hundred million people. These meganations in descending order of population size include China, India, USA, Indonesia, Brazil, Pakistan, Nigeria, Bangladesh, Russia, Japan, and Mexico. Extending the argument one step farther, we note that twenty-five nations have populations in excess of fifty million and that 73 percent of us live in one of those countries.

Most of these meganations have highly centralized relatively undemocratic governments, such as is the case with the United States, China, and Russia. The United States is an autocracy disguised as a democracy but controlled by Wall Street, corporate America, and various foreign interests. While pretending to be a democracy, the US engages in the rendition of terrorist suspects, prisoner abuse and torture, the suppression of civil liberties, citizen surveillance, full-spectrum dominance, and imperial overstretch. Its president has even granted himself the authority to order the assassination of anyone, anywhere, anytime, with no questions asked, no trial, no due process—just pure law of the jungle.

In addition, since the end of World War II, a plethora of highly centralized, undemocratic international megainstitutions have evolved to deal with such issues as national security, peacekeeping, international finance, economic development, and international trade. They include the United Nations, the World Trade Organization, the World Bank, the International Monetary Fund, the European Union, and NATO. What these institutions have in common is not that they are too big to fail, rather they are too big to fix.

No doubt the implosion of the Soviet Union in 1991 and the breakup of Yugoslavia have contributed to the self-determination dynamic in Europe. Active separatist movements can now be found in Bavaria, Belgium, Bulgaria, England, Italy, Lapland, Poland, Romania, Scotland, and Spain. The situation has been exacerbated by the stagnant European economy, the fall of the euro, and increasing doubts about the European Union itself.

Scotland (UK), Flanders (Belgium), and Catalonia (Spain) are the most high-profile self-determination movements in Europe. The Scottish National Party has called for a 2014 referendum on Scottish independence. Recent elections in Catalonia provided additional momentum for a near-term referendum on Catalan self-determination. Last year Belgium went 535 days without a properly elected leader because of the toxicity in the relationship between the wealthier Dutch-speaking Flanders majority and the poorer French-speaking Flemish minority.

In Asia, Bangladesh, China, Myanmar (twelve), India, Indonesia, Japan, and Pakistan all have political independence movements. Hong Kong, Tibet, and Xinjiang are the best-known self-determination movements in China. Kurdish separatists can be found in Iraq, Turkey, and Iran. Indonesia granted East Timor its independence several years ago and also reached an agreement with Aceh that led to its dropping its claim for self-determination and eventually resulted in its dissolution. India is also awash with separatist movements even though secession is illegal there.

Hundreds of African tribes are trying to shake off artificial boundaries imposed on them by nineteenth-century European colonialism. Igbo, Ijaw, Ogani, and Yoruba are all separatist movements located in Nigeria. Sudan recently split into two parts.

For reasons not entirely clear, there seems to be less interest in Latin America in self-determination and political independence than in any other part of the world. Although there are a half dozen or so separatist movements in Brazil, such as the City of São Paulo, the United States of Northeast, and Rio Grande do Sul, one does not have the impression that any of these groups are going anywhere. The one exception to the rule in Latin America is the Zapatista movement in the State of Chiapas in Mexico, the poorest state in the country. Since the 1990s, under the leadership of Subcommandante Marcos and the Zapatista Army of National Liberation (EZLN), the Zapatistas have sought to transform Chiapas into an autonomous self-governing region that supports the political rights of Mexico's native Indian population.

After a near miss in its 1995 referendum to achieve independence from Canada, the Quebec separatist movement fell into the doldrums for over fifteen years. However, in September 2012 the Parti Québécois won a victory of sorts in the Quebec provincial election and was able to put together a weak coalition government. The stability of the new government remains somewhat in doubt. There are also self-determination movements in Alberta and British Columbia.

As for the United States, for over twenty years I have argued that it was too big to manage and should be broken up. On October 9, 1990, three years before I moved to Vermont, the

Bennington Banner published my piece entitled "Should the US Be Downsized?" In 1997 William H. Willimon and I published *Downsizing the USA*, which called for Vermont independence and the peaceful dissolution of the American empire. We argued that not only was the US government too big but that it had become too centralized, too powerful, too undemocratic, too militaristic, too imperialistic, too materialistic, and too unresponsive to the needs of individual citizens and small communities. However, since we were in the midst of the greatest economic boom in history, few Americans were interested in downsizing anything. The name of the game was "up, up, and away." Only bigger and faster were thought to be better.

Prior to September 11, 2001, my call for Vermont self-determination and dissolution of the empire fell mostly on deaf ears. It was as though I were speaking to an audience of one, namely myself. But George W. Bush's ill-conceived, myopic, militaristic response to 9/11 created a window of opportunity to broach the subject of Vermont independence with left-leaning libertarians who might be receptive to the idea. Against the backdrop of the 2003 war with Iraq, we launched the Second Vermont Republic on October 11, 2003.

The Second Vermont Republic is a nonviolent citizens' network and think tank committed to (1) the peaceful breakup of meganations such as the United States, Russia, and China; (2) the political independence of breakaway states such as Quebec, Scotland, and Vermont; and (3) a strategic alliance with other small, democratic, nonviolent, affluent, socially responsible, cooperative, egalitarian, sustainable, ecofriendly nations such as Austria, Finland, and

Switzerland that share a high degree of environmental integrity and a strong sense of community.

There are four reasons supporters of SVR want to secede: First, the US government has lost its moral authority. It is owned, operated, and controlled by Wall Street, corporate America, and the Likud Government of Israel. Second, the US is unsustainable economically, environmentally, socially, morally, and politically. Third, it is too big to govern, as is illustrated by congressional gridlock. Fourth, it is, therefore, unfixable. Few Vermonters are enthralled by a White House that is obsessed with drones, death squads, F-35s, and kill lists.

By the time George W. Bush left office in 2009, there were at least thirty separatist movements in the United States. No doubt the secession petition drive has injected new life into all these self-determination movements. The secession petition for Texas alone contains over 120,000 signatures. A dozen or so of the state petitions have over 25,000 signatures, the number required to trigger a White House response.

Could it be that Americans have not only rediscovered the right of self-determination but also the American Declaration of Independence as well? "Whenever any form of government becomes destructive … it is the right of the people to alter or to abolish it, and to institute a new government." Alteration and abolishment include the right to disband or subdivide or withdraw or create a new government.

So, how is it possible that on the one hand there are nearly a dozen highly centralized meganations whose populations are spiraling upward, while simultaneously over 250 self-determination movements worldwide aspire to split off from megastates such as China, India, Russia, and the United States?

Strange as it may seem, the field of thermodynamics may shed some light on the issue, notwithstanding the fact that I considered it to be the most obscure subject I ever studied when I was a student in the Columbia University School of Engineering back in the late 1950s.

According to the second law of thermodynamics, heat will always flow only from a hotter object to a colder object. More generally, the direction of spontaneous change in isolated systems of all sorts is always toward maximum disorder. This concept is known as *entropy*. Therefore, it is hardly surprising that large, highly centralized, undemocratic nations such as the United States, China, Russia, and India are starting to come unglued at the seams and will eventually descend into chaos.

The economic, financial, social, and political implications of all of this disorder could prove to be staggering. It could also unleash an unprecedented burst of freedom, energy, creativity, and productivity.

We are truly entering unchartered waters. Past trends are meaningless. There are no books or articles available to tell one how to navigate one's ship through the turbulence created by a sea of secession movements.

December 3, 2012

The Montpelier Manifesto

Thomas Naylor

Petition of Grievances

We, citizens of this American land, haunted by the nihilism of separation, meaninglessness, and powerlessness, subsumed by political elites who use corporate, state, and military power to manipulate our lives, pawns of a global system of dominance and deceit in which transnational megacompanies and big government control us through money, markets, and media, sapping our political will, civil liberties, collective memory, traditional cultures, sustainability, and independence, and as victims of affluenza, technomania, cybermania, globalism, and imperialism, do issue and proclaim this:

Document of Grievances and Abuses

Governance
1. A government too big, too centralized, too undemocratic, too unjust, too powerful, too intrusive, and too unresponsive to the needs of individual citizens and small communities.
2. One that is too big and corrupt to be fixed or reformed, certainly not by such fantasies as campaign finance reform or corporate-personhood amendments.
3. One that has lost its moral authority, is corrupt to the core, and

is owned, operated, and controlled by Wall Street, corporate America, and their political lackeys.
4. One run by a single brain-dead national political party on life-support systems, sustained by national and congressional elections that are sold to the highest bidder, disguised as a genuine two-party system.
5. One that relies on and fosters the illusion that only the US government can solve all our problems all the time, in the face of the fact that it is the US government that is the problem.

Economy
1. A collapsing economy, with a moribund housing market and a staggering number of mortgage foreclosures and high unemployment because of jobs lost to China, India, and elsewhere over the past three decades of globalism.
2. Stagnant real incomes for all but the superrich, resulting in an ever-widening gap between the rich and the poor and an increasing rate of poverty, homelessness, and inadequate insurance.
3. A more than $15-trillion national debt and unfunded mandate obligations of $43 trillion, a staggering burden only added to by stimulus spending, tax cuts, and "quantitative easing" (printing money), none of which is restoring economic growth but does make us increasingly and dangerously dependent on China, Japan, and other foreign countries buying our treasury bonds.
4. A central bank that has, by monetizing the growing national debt and providing cheap credit to bail out banks, increased

the money supply to the point where the future value of the dollar and the rate of inflation are highly uncertain.
5. A financial system based on "tricks and traps" rather than customer service and a financial regulatory system that favors predatory and ruthless Wall Street megabanks at the expense of ordinary citizens.
6. An economic system absolutely dependent for survival on consumption and affluenza (the illusion that the accumulation of more stuff, provided by big-box stores fostered by government globalization policies, can provide meaning to life), despite the knowledge that unrestrained growth in a world of finite resources is unsustainable and unworthy of pursuit.
7. Public- and private-sector labor unions that have been under open attack by the government since the Reagan administration, by hostile anti-union private employers such as Walmart and more recently by some Republican governors.
8. Corporate-owned, government-subsidized agriculture, with its use of toxic pesticides and fertilizers, antibiotics, genetically engineered seeds, systematic animal cruelty, and virtual absence of food safety regulations creating a menace to public health, the environment, and small farmers.

Foreign Policy

1. An immoral, often clandestine and illegal, imperial system based on full-spectrum dominance, military overstretch, might makes right, and the proposition that the world wants to be just like us, leading us to provide support to dictators

and authoritarian regimes in the Middle East, North Africa, and elsewhere.

2. A dependence on military might, based on a multitrillion-dollar budget, 1.6 million American troops stationed at over one thousand bases in 153 countries (including eighty thousand in Europe, thirty-six thousand in Japan, and thirty thousand in Korea), Special Operations strike forces (Seals, Delta Forces, Rangers, Green Berets) deployed in 120 countries, and a proliferation of pilotless drone aircraft worldwide for reconnaissance and stealth attacks, sometimes killing civilians, including Americans.

3. Immoral, illegal, undeclared wars in Afghanistan, Pakistan, Somalia, Yemen, and (via Israel) Palestine, the threat of war with Iran based on our deliberate acts of provocation, and the endless "war" on terror largely aimed with racial overtones at Muslims.

4. The hammerlock hold of the Israeli Lobby over American foreign policy that forces us to support an Israeli-inspired war on terror against Muslims and keeps us from any real commitment to an Israeli-Palestinian peace process.

5. The Cuban embargo.

Civil Liberties

1. The highly intrusive, inept, ever-growing, money-guzzling Department of Homeland Security, together with other intelligence agencies, using the Patriot Act, the Military Commissions Act, the Detainee Security Provision of the National Defense Administration Act of 2011, and other covers for citizen surveillance and suppression of civil liberties.

2. The disgraceful (and expensive and useless) Guantanamo Prison, prisoner abuse and torture, and the illegal rendition of terrorist suspects.
3. A president who can order the assassination of anyone, anywhere, anytime (including US citizens) whose name happens to appear on the White House "kill list."

Criminal Justice
1. Six million people under "correctional supervision" (more than were in the Gulag Archipelago under Stalin), including more black men than were in slavery in 1860, and fifty thousand men in solitary confinement in "supermax" prisons.
2. A failed international war on drugs that costs billions, ruins more lives than it saves, has spawned corruption and violence and an entrenched bureaucracy, and has had no impact on drug use in the United States.

Social Services
1. The most expensive health care system in the world, driven by fear of death on the demand side and greed on the supply side, that ranks thirty-seventh in the world according to the World Health Organization, now tied to Obamacare, which remains fatally attached to a private health care system that is in a death-spiral of rising costs and declining health outcomes.
2. An education system dominated by the federal government, committed to a one-size-fits-all corporate model, to the dumbing-down of America, and to a race to the bottom, which is why it ranks eighteenth in the industrial world, according to the OECD.

3. A higher education system that is becoming so expensive that only the rich will be able to attend college.
4. A social-welfare net that, despite being enormously expensive, is woefully inadequate to those it serves and that has proven incapable of serious reform.

Infrastructure

1. A widespread aging and collapsing infrastructure, including highways, bridges, tunnels, airports, dams, levees, and public water systems, now costing America $129 billion a year, according to the American Society of Civil Engineers, and will take an expenditure of $206 billion a year for the next twenty years to fix, sums which are simply unavailable.
2. Transportation crises, including the obsolete and inadequate air-traffic-control systems and railroad passenger train systems, and a federal highway system now sixty years old and falling into disrepair across the country.

Redress of Grievances

"Whenever any form of government becomes destructive ... it is the right of the people to alter or to abolish it, and to institute new government ... as to them shall seem most likely to affect their safety and happiness," says the Declaration of Independence. Alteration and abolishment include the right to disband, or subdivide or withdraw or create a new government.

Let us therefore consider ways to peaceably withdraw from the American empire by (1) regaining control of our lives from big government, big business, big cities, big schools, and big computer networks; (2) relearning how to take care of ourselves by decentralizing, downsizing, localizing, demilitarizing, simplifying, and humanizing our lives; and (3) providing democratic and human-scale self-government at those local and regional levels most likely to affect our safety and happiness.

Citizens, lend your names to this manifesto and join in the honorable task of rejecting the immoral, corrupt, decaying, dying, failing American empire and seeking its rapid and peaceful dissolution before it takes us all down with it.

Thomas H. Naylor
Kirkpatrick Sale
James Starkey
Chellis Glendinning
Carolyn Chute
Charles Keil

This was presented at the Third Statewide Convention on Vermont Self-Determination on September 14, 2012, which was held in the Vermont state house in Montpelier.

Thomas H. Naylor is founder of the Second Vermont Republic and professor emeritus of economics at Duke University.

Kirkpatrick Sale is the author of *Human Scale* and eleven other books and is director of the Middlebury Institute.

James Starkey is professor emeritus of economics at the University of Rhode Island.

Chellis Glendinning is the author of five books, including *When Technology Wounds*, an advisor to SVR, and lives in Cochabamba, Bolivia.

Carolyn Chute is an award-winning Maine novelist, political activist, and author of the best-seller *The Beans of Egypt, Maine*.

Charles Keil is professor emeritus of American studies at the State University of New York at Buffalo.

The Eerie Silence of American Lawyers, Clergy, and Academics in Response to the Empire

Thomas Naylor

At the height of the civil rights and anti–Vietnam War movements back in the late 1960s, the political activism of three professional groups contributed significantly to the success of the two movements—lawyers, clergy, and academics. Liberal attorneys challenged the constitutionality and legality of racial segregation as well as the Vietnam War. Mainline Protestant ministers, Catholic priests, and Jewish rabbis raised questions about whether racism and war were compatible with God's will. Academics not only questioned the morality of the war and racial injustice but also the political, economic, social, and psychological consequences of such aberrant behavior.

Forty years later the United States has become the largest, wealthiest, most powerful, most materialistic, most environmentally irresponsible, most racist, most militaristic, most violent empire in history—an empire whose foreign policy is based on full-spectrum dominance, military overstretch, might makes right, and the proposition that the rest of the world wants to be just like us. And what has been the response of these three professions to this egregious behavior? Stony silence. They appear to be asleep, just like the German people described by Albert Camus in the French resistance newspaper *Combat* in 1944. "Their sleep is filled with nightmares and anxiety, but they are sleeping. We have awaited their awakening for so long, yet they continue to remain stolid, stubborn, and silent as to the crimes committed in their names, as if the entire world and its own destiny had become alien to them."

For the most part, American lawyers and law schools have virtually ignored the Islamophobic war on terrorism, the rendition of terrorist suspects, prisoner abuse and torture, the suppression of civil liberties, and citizen surveillance carried out by the US government. Furthermore, they don't seem to have noticed that the White House can now order the assassination of anyone, anywhere, anytime, who shows up on the White House kill list—no questions asked, no trial, no due process. A far cry from the days of Thurgood Marshall, William Kunstler, Robert Kennedy, and Barbara Jordan.

High-profile religious leaders such as Rev. Martin Luther King Jr., Yale Chaplain William Sloane Coffin, theologian Reinhold Niebuhr, and Rev. Andrew Young were at the forefront of the movements to end racial injustice and the war in Vietnam. Today's sheeplike churches are so docile, so timid, so complacent, so accommodating, and so self-serving that they appear to be more interested in celebrating the hedonism, idolatry, blasphemy, and violence of the American empire rather than condemning it. The state has become the real God of most Americans, which protects our cherished "American way of life."

And the political ferment that rocked college and university campuses in the late 1960s has been replaced by the silent hum of a smooth-running machine tightly controlled by corporate America and the empire itself, both of which wield far more influence on campus than one could have ever imagined might be possible. Today's college campuses are all about keeping their clients happy, political correctness, outside funding, not rocking the boat, and trying to position graduates so they can find a job in an increasingly uncertain job market. Political and economic market conditions define the agenda for the academy. One sometimes wonders if the objective is not to prepare students for the world of technofascism—affluenza, technomania, cybermania, megalomania, robotism, globalization, and imperialism. What ever happened to the Howard Zinns, Carl Sagans, and Kenneth Bouldings of the world?

So long as the nation's best legal, theological, and academic minds are either in a state of denial or complete indifference over the fact that the United States has become an empire capable of inflicting great harm on its citizens as well as the rest of the world, then we are truly in a perilous position. It gives further credence to the argument that not only has our nation lost its moral authority but it is unsustainable, ungovernable, and unfixable.

With such an important part of our country's intellectual firepower sitting silently on the sidelines, we are actually in a far worse position than might first appear. We are morally, spiritually, and intellectually bankrupt.

How all of this will play out in terms of the empire's endgame remains to be seen. But there is no reason to believe it will be a very pretty picture!

November 14, 2012

Thomas Naylor, RIP

Kirkpatrick Sale

Thomas Naylor—he would cringe at anyone calling him "Tom"—was an extraordinary man, and his spirit and his influence will be missed by many.

Thomas died recently of heart failure, in Vermont, the state he and his Second Vermont Republic organization dreamed of having secede from the American empire he so loved to hate. It's doubtful if that group will continue without him, but the Vermont Commons folks and like-minded others will keep the dream alive.

I first met Thomas around 2000, when we both attended a seminar chaired by Donald Livingston, the Emory philosophy professor, to discuss the seminal work of Leopold Kohr, *The Breakdown of Nations*, for which I had written a fond introduction. Around a table of academic right-wingers, with more than a whiff of neoconservative about them, he was the only one to unreservedly understand and appreciate the book and its compelling proof of the desirability and necessity of small nations. We hit it off immediately, of course, and in the course of that weekend, I came to know his authenticity, perspicacity, and kindness.

We corresponded a bit, and then in late 2003, when John Papworth, editor of the *Fourth World Review* in England, was looking around for a place to hold his next Radical Consultation meeting, I suggested Thomas, and John immediately lined him up for a meeting in Vermont for the next year. Thomas had already started his Second Vermont Republic, an organization of mostly himself working to create a separate state for Vermont as it had been between 1777 and 1791, and he agreed to devote the meeting to a discussion of (and we hoped commitment to) secession. We eventually met in Middlebury in early November (the earliest date after the leaf-viewing season when we could afford the rooms) and devoted two days to answering the question of what serious people committed to really changing the government we suffer under and creating societies responsive to human needs could actually do in the world.

We began, naturally, discussing—and shortly dismissing—electoral politics, since no one believed significant change would come out of the present system and present parties—and this was just a few days after Bush had bought himself another presidency. And we took no time in rejecting the reformist lobby-Congress trap that so many liberal groups spend so much time and money on, since that was dealing with those same corrupt parties. Next, we considered the third-party alternative, looking at what effect Perot and Nader had on national affairs—damn little, since the major parties control the system—and concluded that any participation in a corrupt electoral system simply leads to having to be beholden to the same special interests that the major parties are.

What alternatives were left? Well, reform and revolution, of course, and we had a few people championing that, but it didn't take long to realize that all the power was on the other side and they wouldn't be afraid to use it, while a guerrilla uprising figured to be costly and futile as well.

That, naturally, leaves only secession, and Thomas was an

able champion here in putting forth this to people, most of whom had not even thought of this as an alternative before this session. He tended to stress what I came to call the "push" reasons for secession—that is, it allows a state to get out from under an inept, dysfunctional, and evil empire so as not to go down with its inevitable collapse and frees it from the taxes, wars, regulations, and entangling alliances of that empire. I favored more the "pull" reasons—that is, the benefits the state would get if it was on its own, able to gain some measure of democracy, some hands-on control over the decisions that affects its life, in matters such as fuel, food, and finances, some sense of independence and self-determination.

It was not a super easy sell, since many of these people had more anarchistic tendencies, pointing out the difficulties of trying to run any government no matter how small, but in the end almost everyone came around. At the end of the day, we issued a Middlebury Declaration saying, in part:

> The principle of secession must be established as valid and legitimate. To this end, therefore, we are pledged to create a movement that will place secession on the national agenda, encourage nonviolent secessionist organizations throughout the country ... and create a body of scholarship to examine and promote the ideas and principles of secession.

And thus, Thomas Naylor, in effect, created the secession movement and gave impetus to its growing influence over the next decade.

Thomas never wavered from his support for the movement and particularly the Vermont part of it, but he would have his causes and his strategies within it that, once they caught his attention, he would carry on with a passion.

That led him, for example, to meet up with some people who remembered when Scott and Helen Nearing were setting up their homestead in Vermont, and when he studied Scott's writings he found enough of the fierce independence fire (despite the underlying Marxism) to convince him that Nearing was a fitting symbol for the Second Vermont Republic—and anyway, that ought to bring the radicals and the liberals, not to mention back-to-the-landers, into the movement. He somehow met up with a man in Long Island capable of making silver coins, and wouldn't you know that within a few months the SVR website was offering fifty-dollar coins with Nearing's image on one side and a Vermont flag on the other. That the first five hundred of these sold out did nothing to convince some of us that Nearing, who was a lifelong socialist and moved to Maine after giving up on Vermont, had no more to do with secession than Mickey Mouse, but Thomas's enthusiasm never slacked.

Another of his early passions was the idea of a secessionist think tank. He didn't want to do it himself, having enough trouble figuring how to shape an SVR that wasn't invaded by do-gooders and anarchists and the lot of ex-hippies in search of a cause, so he dumped it on me. I little fancied the idea, but he insisted I was the one for it, and in 2005 I gave in and created the Middlebury Institute "for the study of separation, secession, and self-determination," a grand-sounding affair that was nothing more than a website run from my study but was, and remained, a beacon for those interested in examining the subject. Thanks in part to Thomas's urging, I sponsored three national congresses of secessionist organization from around the country (at various times there were as many as thirty-five operating), gaining considerable media attention and putting the movement on the map.

Then in 2011 Thomas read Morris Berman's *Why America Failed*, animated by this vision: "The principal goal of North American civilization, and of its inhabitants, is and always has been an ever-expanding economy—affluence—and endless technological innovation—progress. A nation of hustlers, writes [Walter] McDougall, a people relentlessly on the make." That was right down Thomas's pike, and he wrote a glowing review (as did I, of course) and began to mull over a manifesto that would, in effect, detail how America had profoundly failed as a nation of hustlers and how its present empire was beyond redemption.

That eventually became—after contributions from many people and a rewrite by me (it's what I do)—the Montpelier Manifesto, issued at and endorsed by an independence convention at the Vermont state house earlier this year. Its introduction will give some idea of how it captured much of Thomas's vision:

> We, citizens of this American land, haunted by the nihilism of separation, meaninglessness, and powerlessness, subsumed by political elites who use corporate, state, and military power to manipulate our lives, pawns of a global system of dominance and deceit in which transnational megacompanies and big government control

us through money, markets, and media, sapping our political will, civil liberties, collective memory, traditional cultures, sustainability, and independence, and as victims of affluenza, technomania, cybermania, globalism, and imperialism, do issue and proclaim this Document of Grievances and Abuses.

That was Thomas through and through, in his fullest push mode. But the manifesto ends with a nod to the pull factor:

Let us therefore consider ways to peaceably withdraw from the American empire by (1) regaining control of our lives from big government, big business, big cities, big schools, and big computer networks; (2) relearning how to take care of ourselves by decentralizing, downsizing, localizing, demilitarizing, simplifying, and humanizing our lives; and (3) providing democratic and human-scale self-government at those local and regional levels most likely to affect our safety and happiness.

Thomas's newest passion, and one that alas he did not live to see through, was a conference gathering as many small nations as possible to discuss their important status in the world as balances to the megastates and set up an ongoing organization to keep up a steady criticism of those megastates and empires and to encourage small nations and small nations-to-be—like, for example, Vermont. He had formulated this passion while reading a book by the prince of Liechtenstein, Hans-Adam II, on the importance of the world's smallest states, of which his was one of the smallest (and wealthiest), and so of course he wrote a review of the book (including a criticism of the prince's favorable view of the American empire) and sent it off to the prince.

That began a several-week correspondence, and in the end the prince agreed to sponsor a small-nation conference exactly as Thomas had envisioned it. He passed the organizing job on to a scholar who runs the Liechtenstein Institute of Self-Determination in Princeton that he'd established a few years prior, and there was every reason to think that a conference might be held by the end of next year. Thomas and I talked about it on the phone several times, and he was sure that this would be the instrument finally to stick it to the American empire and gain worldwide backing for the secession movement here and elsewhere.

He won't live to see it, but his colleagues in Vermont and I, with the help of the Liechtenstein institute and the prince, are determined to make it come off, in memory of Thomas, of course, but also because like most of what Thomas did in his life, it is a good and necessary and ultimately important cause.

We will miss him.

December 24, 2012

Afterword: The Pull Factors

Charlie Keil

The less you are and the less you express of your life—the more you have and the greater is your alienated life.

—*Karl Marx*

If we are to reach real peace in this world and if we are to carry on a real war against war, we shall have to begin with children; and if they will grow up in their natural innocence, we won't have to struggle, we won't have to pass fruitless idle resolutions. But we shall go from love to love and peace to peace, until at last all the corners of the world are covered with that peace and love for which, consciously or unconsciously, the whole world is hungering.

—*Gandhi (Young India, November 19, 1931)*

I favored more the pull reasons—that is, the benefits the state would get if it was on its own, able to gain some measure of democracy, some hands-on control over the decisions that affect its life, in matters such as fuel, food, and finances, some sense of independence and self-determination.

—*Kirkpatrick Sale*

Let us therefore consider ways to peaceably withdraw from the American empire by (1) regaining control of our lives from big government, big business, big cities, big schools, and big computer networks; (2) relearning how to take care of ourselves by decentralizing, downsizing, localizing, demilitarizing, simplifying, and humanizing our lives; and (3) providing democratic and human-scale self-government at those local and regional levels most likely to affect our safety and happiness.
—Montpelier Manifesto

These last two pull statements are qualified (*some* measure, *some* hands-on, *some* sense of independence) and abstract. Which "simplifications"? How the hell do we "demilitarize"? How do we "humanize"? Big is bad, unstable, and bound to fail, but how small do we have to go to be good, safe, sane, and successful?

As an anthropologist it's my job to remind readers that all human life was "purely local" or "roaming local" for a few hundred thousand years. It was via mobile gathering egalitarian bands that we coevolved our big brains, opposable thumbs, our *species being* as *Homo ludens collaborans*. My Hessian grandmother knew about the spirits in trees, so my children are just three generations removed from paganism, animism, and nature worship. Not just "once upon a time" but for all of prehistory and most of history, all of human time until this past century or so, we (almost all of us) lived in thousands of different egalitarian societies with thousands of different languages, myths, tree spirits, and song and dance styles. Even as we began to settle down in compounds, small hamlets, and villages, each settlement probably had its own ways of drumming, unique tunings of log xylophones, and special instruments like homemade flutes and "finger pianos" that were "personal" and not standardized. That's what I found in Eha Amufu in Eastern Nigeria in 1960, when I was twenty and Nigeria was on the eve of independence. I immediately turn to personal and small group ways of playing instruments, making what Westerners call "music," because I believe that the pull factors moving us toward sustainable, resilient, peaceful, and prosperous living are primarily and most powerfully spiritual, soulful, philosophical, sonic, rhythmic, and satisfying culturally because we will be moving and grooving to build and enjoy unique expressions of cultural pattern that tell our children who we are, where we are, why we are, in places we belong to … and that do not really belong to us as "private property."

Yes, we will become groups of people who belong to the land and watershed they occupy as "land trusts" and "water commons" but do not own. Our true species being—*Homo ludens collaborans*, humorous-playful-collaborator—requires modes of social being in very great, if not infinite, variety. Each person, each immediate family, each small group of friends and players (in combos and "*parees*"[7]), each extended family, each small settlement or neighborhood, each watershed or bioregional population, each county/canton/province, requires and acquires an amusing, fun-filled, and playful identity of its own. "Amusing" in the sense of each person and group, not merely invoking but embodying Mother Memory and her nine daughters, the muses, in a unique way. This is how the people in each culture will know if each person and every group is,

---

7 *parea* (s.), *parees* (pl.): Greek words for small, intense, conversation-crazy, friendship groups.

in fact, self-determined and self-determining. Is each person happily self-expressed within each *kulturkreis* or "culture circle" they inhabit?

How else will each child come to know and recognize who he or she is part of ... safe with ... innocent in the company of ... happy to jam with? It takes a whole child to become a healthy, fully expressed, creative genius within a healthy resilient village. Are you, gentle reader, in the process of creating such a village, commune, neighborhood, block club, book club, or social aid and pleasure club (the organizations that sponsor Sunday parades in New Orleans)?

There is a rapidly growing shelf of readings to help you. And, of course, our third volume, *Reclaiming Social Being* (in our series, *Local Paths to Peace Today*), is coming your way soon.

Update: May 15, 2018

At the moment, secessionist flood waters are rising, but the floodgates are not opening. The right to self-determination of persons and peoples is not a great and common theme of human development, but it's happening anyway. Peoples all over the world will be helping this process along and also holding each self-determining person accountable—for not polluting any headwaters on the land they belong to; not using up or damming up streams or rivers without full permission from everyone downstream and a sign from the Mother; for not increasing their population beyond the carrying capacity of the land they belong to; for examining every new technology closely before licensing it to be marketed; for inventing more religious or spiritual or cultural orientations that enable people to work less and play more. This list of "do no harm" limits and boundaries needs to be long, extended as necessary, and detailed at the start of our transition from a legal world back to the natural world but can be continually shortened as we achieve world peace, regional peace, and regain ecoequilibrio in every region and locality.

States all over the world are still attempting to ethnic cleanse, to commit genocide, to suppress, manipulate, and expel peoples, and to suppress, oppress, censor, purge, and expel persons. The big state powers—USA, Russia, China—support and approve it routinely and ruthlessly, and lesser state powers—Sudan, Burma/Myanmar, Rwanda, Serbia, Nigeria, etc.—do it whenever they think they can get away with it.

But now we are back to that way-too-long list of factors pushing us to create a world that is safe and joyous for the children of our species and for all the other life-forms we have been coevolving with since time immemorial. The powerful and wonderful pull factors are something you can discover and nurture wherever you happen to be living.

Organizations I've supported

As a war tax resistor in the late 1960s and again from 2008 to the present, I have enjoyed giving away over half my income each year to organizations that support peace, ecological balance, health, and women's and children's liberation. Here is a list of charitable 501(c)(3) organizations that you can contribute to with some confidence that almost every penny will be spent on people and practices that will bring us closer to decentralized peace, ecoequilibrio, and egalitarian styles of voluntary lower-middle-classness within thriving local peace economies.

350.org—https://350.org

A. J. Muste Memorial Institute—https://ajmuste.org

Alliance for Childhood—http://www.allianceforchildhood.org

American Friends Service Committee—https://www.afsc.org

Code Pink—https://www.codepink.org

Corporate Accountability International—https://www.corporateaccountability.org

Democracy Now!—https://www.democracynow.org

Doctors Without Borders—https://www.doctorswithoutborders.org

Earthjustice—https://earthjustice.org

Fellowship of Reconciliation—https://www.forusa.org

Friends of the Earth—https://foe.org

Green Horizon Foundation—http://green-horizon.org/donat/

Greenpeace Fund—https://www.greenpeacefund.orgs

Humane Farming Association—https://www.hfa.org

Honkfest! (via Great Small Works)—http://honkfest.org/help/

Iraq Veterans Against the War—http://www.ivaw.org

Jubilation Foundation—http://jubilationfoundation.org

Liberty Tree Foundation (backs up Green Party thinking, education)—https://www.libertytreefoundation.org

National War Tax Resistance Coordinating Committee (via "ROSC")—https://nwtrcc.org

Nuclear Age Peace Foundation—https://www.wagingpeace.org

Organic Consumers Association—https://www.organicconsumers.org

Oxfam—https://www.oxfamamerica.org

Peace Tax Fund—http://peacetaxfund.org

Peace Development Fund—https://www.peacedevelopmentfund.org

Peace Action Education Fund—https://www.peaceaction.org

Physicians for Human Rights—http://physiciansforhumanrights.org

Planned Parenthood—https://www.plannedparenthood.org

Public Citizen Foundation—https://www.citizen.org

Schumacher Center for New Economics—http://www.centerforneweconomics.org

Sierra Club Foundation (for Law Program and Foundation)—https://www.sierraclubfoundation.org/what-we-fund/environmental-law-program

Transition US—http://www.transitionus.org

Union of Concerned Scientists—https://www.ucsusa.org

Western NY Land Conservancy—https://wnylc.org

War Resisters League (support via A. J. Muste Memorial Institute)—https://www.warresisters.org

World Beyond War (David Swanson)—https://worldbeyondwar.org

The Books of Thomas H. Naylor

Linear Programming (with Eugene Byrne), Belmont, CA: Wadsworth Publishing Company, 1963.

Computer Simulation Techniques (with Joseph L. Balintfy, Donald S. Burdick, and Kong Chu). New York: John Wiley and Sons, 1966. Translated into Japanese, Portuguese, and Spanish.

The Impact of the Computer on Society (editor). Atlanta: Southern Regional Education Board, 1967.

Microeconomics and Decision Models of the Firm (with John Vernon). New York: Harcourt, Brace, and World, 1969. Translated into Spanish.

The Design of Computer Simulation Experiments (editor). Durham, NC: Duke University Press, 1969.

Introduction to Linear Programming (with Eugene Byrne and John Vernon). Belmont, CA: Wadsworth Publishing Co., 1971. Paperback edition, 1975.

Computer Simulation Experiments with Models of Economic Systems. New York: John Wiley and Sons, 1971. Translated into Spanish, Polish, and Russian.

You Can't Eat Magnolias (editor with H. Brandt Ayers). New York: McGraw-Hill, 1972.

Strategies for Change in the South (with James Clotfelter). Chapel Hill, NC: University of North Carolina Press, 1975.

SIMPLAN: A Planning and Modeling System for Government (with Harold Glass, David Milstein, and John Wall). Durham, NC: Duke University Press, 1977.

The Politics of Corporate Planning and Modeling (editor). Oxford, OH: Planning Executives Institute, 1978.

Corporate Planning Models. Reading, MA: Addison-Wesley, 1979.

Simulation Models in Corporate Planning (editor). New York: Praeger Press, 1979,

Strategic Planning Management. Oxford, OH: Planning Executives Institute, 1980.

Simulation in Business Planning and Decision Making (editor). LaJolla, CA: The Society for Computer Simulation, 1981.

Corporate Strategy: The Integration of Corporate Planning Models and Economics (editor). Amsterdam: North-Holland, 1982.

Computer Based Planning Systems (editor with Michele H. Mann). Oxford, OH: Planning Executives Institute, 1982.

Managerial Economics: Corporate Economics and Strategy (with John M. Vernon and Kenneth Wertz). New York: McGraw-Hill, 1983.

Portfolio Planning and Corporate Strategy (editor with Michele H. Mann). Oxford, OH: Planning Executives Institute, 1983.

Optimization Models for Strategic Planning (editor with Celia Thomas). Amsterdam: North-Holland, 1984.

The Corporate Strategy Matrix. New York: Basic Books, 1986. Translated into Hungarian.

The Gorbachev Strategy: Opening the Closed Society. Lexington, MA: Lexington Books, 1988.

The Cold War Legacy. Lexington, MA: Lexington Books, 1991.

The Search for Meaning (with William H. Willimon and Magdalena R. Naylor). Nashville: Abingdon Press, 1994. Paperback edition, 1997. Translated into Korean.

The Search for Meaning Workbook (with William H. Willimon and Magdalena R. Naylor). Nashville: Abingdon Press, 1994.

The Abandoned Generation: Rethinking Higher Education (with William H. Willimon). Grand Rapids, MI: Wm. B. Eerdmans Publishing, 1995.

The Search for Meaning in the Workplace (with Rolf Österberg and William H. Willimon). Nashville, TN: Abingdon Press, 1996.

Downsizing the USA (with William H. Willimon). Grand Rapids, MI: Wm. B. Eerdmans Publishing, 1997.

Affluenza (with John De Graaf and David Wann). San Francisco, CA: Berrett-Koehler, 2001. Second edition, 2005. Translated into six languages.

The Vermont Manifesto: The Second Vermont Republic. Philadelphia, PA: Xlibris, 2003.

Secession. Port Townsend, WA: Feral House, 2008.

CPSIA information can be obtained
at www.ICGtesting.com
Printed in the USA
BVHW070640091019
560601BV00003B/12/P